the dodo

Rosie's Story

The True Story of a Cat and Her Unlikely Best Friend

BY BONNIE BADER

SCHOLASTIC INC.

All photos © Bui Sisters

Stock Photos © Shutterstock.com

ISBN 978-1-338-84517-4

10 9 8 7 6 5 4 3 2   22 23 24 25 26

Printed in the U.S.A.   40
First printing 2022

Book design by Jennifer Rinaldi

CONTENTS

CHAPTER 1
RESCUED

ON AN APRIL EVENING IN 2015, THI Bui (say: *Tee Boo-ee*) received an urgent call from a friend. A tiny kitten had been found alone on a dark street in San Jose, California. Twenty-two-year-old Thi had been rescuing kittens for a long time, so she sprang into action.

Within minutes, Thi arrived at the scene, where she discovered the kitten curled up on the street outside her friend's house. The kitten had mostly black-and-brown fur, but her paws, legs, and chest were white. She was very tiny indeed.

Thi tucked her strands of long black hair behind her ears and bent down to get a closer look. "She looks sick," she said. "Poor thing."

She looked around for the kitten's mother, but there wasn't another cat in sight. Thi's friend said she hadn't seen another cat for at least a day. Thi knew that without a mother to take care of her, the orphaned kitten would need help to survive.

Thi gently picked up the trembling kitten. "I have to get you home, little one."

"As soon as I saw her, I knew you'd be able to help her," Thi's friend said gratefully.

"Thanks for calling," Thi replied, cradling the long-haired tabby kitten in her arms.

Carefully, Thi laid the kitten on the front seat of her car. She covered her with a blanket to keep her nice and snug. Then Thi began her drive home.

As she pulled up to a stop sign, she glanced at the kitten and smiled.

The kitten yawned, curling her tiny pink tongue.

Although Thi had rescued a lot of kittens in her life, there was something very special about this one. She could just feel it.

The little kitten slowly opened her green eyes. She didn't know where she was. She was shivering, but she was starting to feel warmer now that she was nestled in a cozy blanket. Her stomach grumbled, but there was no mom to feed her.

What's happening? she thought.

The kitten tilted her head and saw someone seated beside her, her hands on a steering wheel. They were inside a car . . . *But where are we headed?* she wondered.

Bump!

The kitten's body jerked, and the person's hand shot out to keep her from flying forward. The kitten sniffed. The hand smelled sweet and comforting. Maybe this human had food for her. Her stomach gurgled again. She opened her mouth, mewling, but no food appeared.

She was starting to feel hungrier and weaker by the second . . .

Thi rushed the kitten inside her single-story house, which was where she and her two sisters,

Thoa (say: *Twa*) and Tram, took care of abandoned animals. The Bui sisters had tons of experience with newborn kittens, so Thi knew just what to do. She started by placing the tiny kitten on a heated blanket.

From the looks of her, the kitten was about two-and-a-half to three weeks old. A kitten that age needed their mother's milk. But since there was no mother cat around, Thi needed to prepare a bottle of kitten formula, which was as close as she was going to get to real cat milk.

"Don't worry," Thi assured the kitten. "I've got something yummy for you."

Thi took the formula out from the closet. Feeding a kitten cow's milk or soy milk can be very dangerous. Luckily, kitten formula has just the right kind of vitamins and minerals that newborn kittens need to help them grow.

And this little one needed the kitten formula right away!

Quickly, Thi fit a special bottle with a rubber tip. These rubber tips make a kitten think they are drinking milk from their mother. If the kitten's mouth is very tiny, a dropper can be used to deliver the milk instead. Whatever the method, Thi knew it was important to make sure the formula drips out one drop at a time. After all, this was a teeny-tiny kitten with a teeny-tiny mouth and a teeny-tiny tummy!

Once the powdered formula and warm water were added to the bottle, Thi shook it to make sure there were no lumps. Clumps of powder can block the hole and keep the kitten from getting the milk. Thi tested the formula on the inside of her wrist to make sure it wasn't too hot, picked the kitten up, and placed her belly down on her lap. This is the safest position to bottle-feed a kitten. This is also the position a kitten would most likely take milk from their mother.

Thi guided the kitten toward the bottle. Slowly, the formula dripped into her hungry mouth.

"There you go. Easy now," Thi said.

Just then, Lilo, one of Thi's huskies, padded into the living room to see what was going on. Lilo had just been spayed and was wearing a cone so that she couldn't bite or lick the itchy stitches.

"Hi, Lilo," Thi said. "Came to see what all the excitement is about, huh?"

Lilo kissed Thi, then glanced at the kitten and trotted back to her bed.

Tram, the youngest Bui sister, passed Lilo in the doorway as she stepped into the living room.

"I see we have another patient," Tram said, kneeling next to Thi and the kitten.

Thi nodded. "My friend called me about this rescue, and I think I got there just in time. This kitten is so frail."

"She must be starving," Tram added. "Speaking of starving, I'll go feed the others." And with that, she headed into the kitchen to prepare bottles for their other little rescue kittens.

Thi's kitten felt something warm and soft touch her mouth, and . . . was that *milk?*

With all the energy she could find, the kitten suckled on the bottle. The warm milk tasted so good after being hungry for so long. As she drank, her tired eyes began to close.

After a few more small sips, she fell fast asleep in her rescuer's lap.

Thi had breathed a sigh of relief when the kitten started taking the bottle. But when the kitten stopped drinking, she grew worried. She knew the kitten needed more than a few sips . . .

"So cute!" said Thoa as she walked into the living room. She pulled out her phone to snap a photo of the little kitten.

Thi nodded. "Cute, but weak. I tried feeding her, but she didn't take much."

Thoa sighed. "She must be exhausted. Who knows what she's been through?"

"We have to do everything we can to try to save her," Thi said. "She needs more milk."

"Agreed." Tram entered the living room to

join in. "First things first: feeding schedule." Tram grabbed a pen and piece of paper. The sisters were used to creating strict round-the-clock schedules for the newborn—or "neonatal"—kittens they rescued.

According to the schedule, the sisters would rotate the feedings every two to three hours, and try to give the tiny kitten ten to fourteen milliliters of formula each time. The sisters knew they wouldn't get much sleep, but they were used to that. It was what they needed to do to keep the kitten alive.

Thoa and Tram retreated back to their rooms to sleep before it was their turn. Meanwhile, Thi held the bottle, waiting for the kitten to wake up and take a sip. Her eyes settled on a photograph of her with her two sisters back in middle school.

Since then, Thi had been taking care of

street cats—also known as "feral" cats. She couldn't bear to see cats without homes, but her mother wouldn't let her bring them inside. So instead she put fresh food and water out for them. But one day, Thi found two neonatal kittens. She knew she couldn't simply leave food outside for them. These little kittens needed extra special care or they wouldn't survive. So, against her mother's wishes, Thi brought them inside the house.

Thi's mother wasn't happy when she saw the kittens crawling across their kitchen floor. She didn't like the idea of feral animals in her house; they are usually scared of humans and may not know how to act around them. But when she looked at the tiny balls of fur and their sweet blue eyes, she couldn't turn them away. She told Thi that she could keep the kittens to nurse.

Was Thi's mother only giving her

permission to bring those two cats in? Thi didn't ask, and from that day on, Thi and her sisters started fostering neonatal kittens at home. Fostering animals means to take care of them temporarily until a forever home is found.

"Come on, little one," Thi urged the kitten, who was still fast asleep on her lap. Thi tickled the kitten's lips with the bottle, but she didn't stir. Thi yawned. It was late. She was exhausted.

"My turn," a sleepy Thoa said as she entered in striped pajamas.

Thi handed the kitten to her sister for the next feeding shift and trudged into her seafoam-green bedroom. She had just plopped down on her bed and had managed to doze off when—

Beep! Beep!

Thi's alarm sounded. Although she was tempted to press snooze and fall back asleep, she knew it was already her turn to feed the kitten again. Thi got up and shuffled sleepily back into the living room.

Tram was sitting with the kitten now, and when she saw Thi, her lip trembled.

Suddenly, Thi felt wide awake. "What's wrong?" she asked her sister.

"The kitten's taken a turn for the worse," Tram said, her eyes filling with tears. "She hasn't had one drop of milk from my bottle, or from Thoa's during her feeding shift earlier. I'm scared."

Thi tried not to panic. Quickly, she rushed into the kitchen to fix a fresh bottle of warm formula. "Tram, can you go wake Thoa?" she called over her shoulder. She tried not to be too loud. She didn't want to wake their mother. "Maybe between the three of us, we can figure out what to do!"

While Tram went to wake Thoa, Thi

scrambled back into the living room and settled down on the comfortable couch, placed the kitten on her belly, and tried to feed her the new bottle.

Nothing.

Thi tried to hold the kitten's head at different angles.

Still nothing.

She tried placing the bottle in different parts of the kitten's mouth.

But no matter what Thi did, the kitten did not take the milk—not a *single* drop.

Thi's eyes welled with tears, looking from Tram to Thoa, who were in the doorway.

Thi sniffled. "What now?"

Tram and Thoa didn't know.

There was only one thing about which Thi was certain: Without milk, the kitten wouldn't make it.

CHAPTER 2
A MATTER OF SURVIVAL

LILO THE HUSKY RETURNED TO THE living room, where Thi sat with the kitten while her sisters slept in their bedrooms.

Lilo sniffed. *Why are you paying attention to that kitten when I need you?*

"Hello, girl. Couldn't sleep?" Thi asked, softly petting Lilo's back. Thi knew Lilo was still very uncomfortable after her surgery.

Lilo tried to get closer to the kitten in Thi's lap, but the cone around her neck stopped her. *Why does this thing keep getting in my way?* Lilo shook her head, but the cone simply wouldn't budge.

Still, even from a distance, Lilo could tell that something was not right.

The kitten was lying very still on Thi's lap. She was barely breathing.

Lilo whimpered—partially because her stitches and cone were making her itch, but also because she was worried about the little kitten, and about Thi, who looked so sad. Thi had brought plenty of kittens home before, but Lilo had never seen Thi look this worried before.

It's okay, Thi, I am here for you. I can make you feel better, Lilo thought. *And maybe I can help this little kitten, too.*

Thi petted Lilo, whose beautiful light brown eyes glanced at the helpless kitten. "Yes, Lilo, this little kitten is very sick."

Lilo nudged Thi's knees with her cone.

Thi smiled. "I know you aren't feeling well, either, but you'll heal soon. I'm not so sure about this one, though." With those last words, Thi's smile disappeared.

Lilo nudged Thi again, and Thi noticed that Lilo's eyes were fixed on the kitten. It was strange, since Lilo—although a kind and loving dog—usually ignored the rescues Thi and her sisters brought home. Why had this one captured Lilo's attention?

"Lilo, sit," Thi commanded. "This kitten isn't well enough to play."

Lilo is a Siberian husky, and huskies

and kittens don't always get along well together. Huskies originated from the polar regions of the world. They are strong and independent dogs, but they can also be stubborn. Plus, they have tons of energy, which was not at all what Thi or the kitten needed at the moment.

Thi softly nudged the kitten's head to try to get her to drink, but she stayed asleep.

"Any luck?" asked a sleepy Tram as she walked into the living room.

Thi shook her head.

"I'm going to take the dogs out for a walk and then I'll take over. Finny!" Tram called to her own pet husky. "Time to go out!"

Finny trotted over, and Tram put on her leash.

Then she held up Lilo's leash, but Lilo was frozen in place.

"What's up with Lilo?" Tram asked. Lilo may have just had surgery, but usually nothing stopped her when it was time for a walk.

Thi shrugged. "You got me. I peeked at her stitches, and they look okay, so I don't think it's that."

"Come on, Lilo, time for a walk," Tram said again.

But Lilo's eyes were glued on the kitten. She wasn't going anywhere.

Finny was growing impatient, and Tram knew that both dogs really needed to go out. Finally, she grabbed a flavorful homemade treat and Lilo reluctantly followed.

But as soon as they came back inside, Lilo ran back to Thi and the kitten.

"Here, let me take a turn sitting with the kitten," Tram told her sister. "And maybe you can get Lilo interested in something else."

Thi got up and stretched. Her body ached. "Come on, Lilo, do you want to play?"

Lilo still couldn't take her eyes off the kitten.

"Well, if Lilo wants to stay with you, I'm going to try to catch some sleep," Thi said.

Tram nodded, and Thi went into her room and lay down. But she couldn't sleep. There was something about this kitten that had gotten to her, although she couldn't figure out exactly what it was.

And why was Lilo so interested in the kitten? She usually just sniffed the rescues and then went about her business. But with this one, there was something different going on.

Thi pulled the covers snug and thought back to when she'd first adopted Lilo as an eight-week-old adorable fluffy puppy. Before bringing Lilo home, Thi did a lot of research.

But no amount of research could have prepared her and her family for Lilo. For starters, she was very mischievous. Whenever they turned their backs, the sisters knew Lilo was going to find trouble—usually by acting wild with one of her toys or getting into something she shouldn't. Plus, she had a habit of guarding her food, and would sometimes growl when the sisters came near her bowl. But they were able to train her not to do this by earning her trust and hand-feeding her meals. No matter what, they loved their puppy so much—and now Lilo knew they loved her back.

In addition to hand-feeding Lilo, the sisters also taught her the "leave it" command. Lilo was a super-fast learner, so she caught onto the new command quickly. She would drop whatever toy or food was in her mouth when Thi and her sisters told her to. When Lilo was nine weeks old, she graduated from puppy school with flying colors. At three months, Lilo started training that used positive reinforcement. Positive reinforcement uses rewards like treats or praise for good behavior.

After a while, Lilo's good behavior became second nature. For months, the Bui sisters worked with Lilo even more on her obedience, recall, and agility. The goal was to get Lilo to complete the Canine Good Citizen program. Through this program, Lilo learned confidence and good manners, both inside and outside her house. Lilo succeeded in this program—in fact, she graduated at the top of her class!

But after Lilo's training, something frightening happened. Another dog pounced and hurt Lilo at a pet store. The incident left Lilo with cuts on her face.

After that, the sisters could no longer take Lilo to her favorite places, like the dog park and the beach. Lilo was suddenly scared of other dogs, and she would sometimes lash out at them. She was still fearful from the pet store incident, and she felt like she had to protect herself. Thi always regretted not jumping in sooner to protect Lilo that day in the pet store. At the same time, she knew there was little she could have done.

From that day on, Lilo's attitude toward other dogs grew worse. The sisters enrolled Lilo in another training school. This school's philosophy was to not have dogs interact with one another. The school was against dog parks, dog beaches, and dog social events. But those were some of Lilo's favorite things! So the sisters decided to leave the school and try something else. Lilo had to learn to be more relaxed around other dogs—but how were they going to train Lilo to do this?

As Thi tossed and turned in her bed, she had a few more thoughts before letting herself drift off. She knew she and her sisters still had to figure out how to help Lilo.

But first, they must figure out how to help the kitten in the other room.

I can help! I really can, Lilo thought, her tail wagging and her eyes fixed on the sweet kitten. She didn't understand why no one would let her get close. If she could just get near enough, Lilo might be able to warm up the kitten with her thick coat of fur and give her the strength she needed.

But no matter how much Lilo whined, the sisters kept the kitten far away from her.

Thi dreamed she and Lilo were hiking in Lake Tahoe, over streams, rocks, and fallen branches.

"Thi?" Thoa's voice from the living room snapped Thi awake.

Was Thoa shouting about the kitten? Was she okay? Thi stumbled out of bed and raced into the living room. It was morning now, and sunlight slanted into the room. Thi rubbed her eyes and approached Thoa cradling the kitten in her lap. And there by her side was Lilo.

"Has she taken any milk?" Thi asked desperately.

Thoa slowly shook her head. She looked

exhausted and scared. "She didn't wake up at all, Thi. I think . . . I think . . ."

Just then, Lilo let out a howl, as if urging the sisters not to give up.

"Do you think Lilo wants to help?" Thi asked Thoa.

"That's ridiculous," Thoa said. "I mean, a husky helping a kitten? What can *she* do?"

Thi looked at the little ball of fur in Thoa's lap and began to cry.

"It's okay," Thoa said, trying to comfort her. "You did your best. We all did."

Lilo ran to Thi and licked her tears. Then she ran over to the kitten and howled again.

"What's all the commotion?" Tram asked, stretching her arms and walking into the room. Her dark hair was pulled into a ponytail, a pair of Rollerblades slung over her shoulder.

"Thi thinks Lilo can help the kitten, and it

kind of seems like Lilo thinks she can help, too," Thoa explained.

Tram's eyes widened. *"Really?"*

"It's our last resort," Thi said. "What do you think?"

Tram thought for a minute. "I say we go for it."

Thi patted Lilo's soft fur.

Lilo looked at Thi with her light eyes. Then Lilo looked at the kitten.

Lilo's fur is so warm and soft, Thi reasoned, *just like a mama cat's fur . . .*

But Lilo was a *husky.*

A *dog.*

Yet the kitten was getting worse by the second. Letting Lilo help was their last chance to save her.

Thi glanced at her sisters, who nodded in agreement. Heart pounding, she nestled the kitten on the ground beside Lilo. She and her sisters held their breath, looking on with wide eyes.

All that was left was to wait and see what Lilo would do.

CHAPTER 3
MOTHER KNOWS BEST

DURING THE FIRST MONTH OF their lives, kittens need their mothers, not only for milk, but also for warmth. Neonatal kittens can't adjust their own body temperatures, so it's vital they have their mothers' fluffy bodies to nuzzle up against like big soft blankets. A mother cat normally provides body heat with temperatures between 100 and 103 degrees Fahrenheit.

Thi and her sisters always make sure to keep their neonatal kittens warm. For example, they build cozy little areas with heating pads covered with fresh and clean blankets or towels.

"Look, the kitten is cuddling right up to Lilo . . ." Tram observed.

But Thi was still feeling nervous.

The kitten might be getting comfortable, but was Lilo?

The kitten sniffed. Then she sniffed again. Something smelled different than the hand that had been trying to feed her. This was a more *earthy* smell. She cracked open her eyes and blinked. She was surrounded by someone else's brown-and-white fur—and lots of it. And it was warm. Nice and warm.

As hungry as she was, the kitten was also sleepy.

She shut her eyes and drifted off.

Lilo didn't move as the kitten slept in her fur.

Then Lilo opened her mouth, revealing her sharp, shiny teeth. Thi panicked. Was Lilo going to bite the kitten? Lilo moved her mouth toward the kitten. Thi moved to stop her when—

"Look! Lilo is licking the kitten!" Thoa exclaimed. "As if she is her own puppy!"

Thi froze, watching in awe as Lilo softly licked the kitten's tiny ears and nose. "Mom, you have to come check this out!" she shouted as her fear turned to excitement. Their mom was always up by now, and Thi could hear her making coffee in the kitchen.

In seconds, Thi's mom rushed in. Together, the family watched the kitten nuzzle into the crook of Lilo's neck. They were cuddling! Lilo closed her eyes and snoozed with the kitten.

Thi's heart swelled with joy. "Lilo is acting like the kitten's mother!"

Everyone gave a silent cheer, followed by a sigh of relief.

This feels nice, Lilo thought as the kitten snuggled up against her. *And I don't know why, but it feels . . . right.* Lilo peeped open her eyes to check on the kitten. She started licking the kitten's coat. Her body was so small and fragile, and Lilo somehow knew she had to be extra gentle.

Meanwhile, Thi was pacing around the two of them.

"Why do you still look so worried?" her mom asked, cocking her head. "The kitten looks comfortable."

Thi gave a heavy sigh. "True, but she still hasn't eaten anything!"

"And neither have you," her mom said, heading into the kitchen to make her some food.

"Mom, it's okay, I'm not very hungry," Thi protested.

But all Thi could hear in response was the clanging of pots and pans.

Suddenly, the kitten stirred. Thi froze and couldn't believe her eyes. "Oh my gosh! The kitten! She's awake!" Thi called.

Thoa and Tram raced into the room and stared in amazement.

"If she's awake, maybe she'll drink the milk now," Thi said. "I'll go make a bottle."

In the kitchen, Thi prepared a fresh bottle and tested the milk on the inside of her wrist again to make sure it wasn't too hot. Perfect! Back on the couch in the living room, she took the kitten, put her in the same position as before, and placed the bottle in her mouth. Everyone crowded around.

"Look! She's drinking!" Thi exclaimed.

"Wow," Tram breathed. "Lilo really helped her! I bet the warmth from Lilo gave her the strength to wake up."

In all their years nursing kittens, the sisters had never seen anything like this.

The kitten drank quickly—the bottle was nearly empty!

"We're not out of the woods just yet," Thi pointed out. "We still have to keep to the feeding schedule. I hope that taking this one bottle wasn't a fluke."

Two hours later, Tram prepared another bottle for the kitten.

She drank that one, too!

And the next bottle, and the next.

During Thi's feeding shift, she noticed Lilo hadn't left the kitten's side the entire time.

"You are such a good girl." Thi ruffled Lilo's fur. "But you need to eat something, too."

Lilo wouldn't budge.

Like a concerned mother, she did not want to leave the kitten—not even to eat her own food! And like a concerned pet parent, Thi brought Lilo's big bowl of kibble over to her.

Lilo gobbled down her food, all the while keeping an eye on the kitten.

Each morning, Thi weighed the kitten on the scale. Daily weighing of a neonatal kitten is very important. If the kitten is gaining weight, it means they are getting proper nutrition. Weighing a kitten each day also provides information about how much the kitten should be fed. If the kitten is not gaining enough weight, they might need more milk with each feeding. A typical kitten gains about one half ounce a day, or four ounces a week. Thankfully, this kitten was finally right on track.

Thi picked up the kitten and gently kissed her. The kitten purred and licked Thi on the nose. Thi giggled. "You scared us, little one, but it looks like you're going to make it." She put the kitten down on the ground, and Lilo trotted over, giving the kitten kisses of her own.

"I think it's time we gave you a name," Thi said.

"Good idea," Thoa said. She had just returned from a run with Finny.

"Tram!" Thi called. "Family meeting!"

Tram poked her head into the room. "What's up?"

"I think it's time we picked a name," Thi said, pulling the kitten onto her lap.

Tram nodded. "Well, since you rescued her, Thi, you should get to name her."

Thi closed her eyes, thinking. They had named so many kittens over the years, but this kitten needed a special name . . .

"She's like a delicate flower," Thi said after a minute. "Maybe Lily. Or Daisy. Or Rose."

Despite Thoa's and Tram's nods of agreement, Thi wasn't completely satisfied.

None of the names were an exact fit.

"I know!" Thi shouted. "Rosie. Something about that name just feels right."

"I love it," said Thoa.

"Come on, Rosie," Tram said, trying out the new name, "it's time for a feeding."

This time, after Rosie drank, Tram decided to try and burp her, in case she swallowed air from the bottle. Just like with a human baby, it isn't good to let air bubbles float in a kitten's stomach. She laid Rosie on her stomach and gently patted her back until she heard a little burp.

Afterward, Rosie snuggled up right next to Lilo.

Lilo was falling into her role as the kitten's substitute mother, continuing to let Rosie nuzzle her. The act seemed to comfort Rosie and, at the same time, made Lilo feel calmer, too.

One day, the sisters sat around watching Lilo and Rosie cuddle.

"Lilo is such a good mama. I should take a video of them," Thoa said with a laugh.

"Wait," Tram said, grabbing her arm. "That's a great idea."

Thoa shook her head. "I was just kidding. Really. I want to save my filmmaking skills for something more serious."

"But this *is* serious," Thi insisted. "I mean who would ever believe that a husky is caring for a neonatal kitten?"

Thoa thought for a minute. "Maybe we should start by posting photos of them online!"

"Yeah!" Tram and Thi said at the same time.

Immediately, the sisters began looking through their phones to find the perfect photos. After they picked them out, they wrote sweet captions and uploaded the pictures to social media.

One photo caption said: *Hush little darling, don't say a word, Mama's gonna buy you a mockingbird.*

One follower wrote: *How adorable is this!! Baby Rosie.*

"Look!" Tram said. "We're getting more followers. People are loving Lilo and Rosie!" Who ever thought that a huge husky and a teeny kitten could form such a bond?

CHAPTER 4
BONDS UNBROKEN

IN THE BACK OF HER MIND, THI couldn't help but wonder what would happen when the day came to find a forever home for Rosie. The sisters' policy was that once their foster kittens grew strong and old enough, they found them a forever home. But what would Lilo do without her little friend?

Still, Thi smiled as she watched Rosie

playing with Lilo. At first, all of Rosie's running around worried Thi. Would it annoy Lilo? But Lilo didn't mind Rosie's antics. In fact, it seemed as though she was encouraging the playful side of Rosie!

Are you my mama? Rosie thought, lightly pawing Lilo's face. *Come on, play with me!* Rosie jumped on top of Lilo's head and looked around the room.

Thi smiled and picked up a long stick with a feather at the end. She put it in front of Rosie's face. Rosie reached out to grab it, but just like that, it was pulled quickly away.

I'm gonna get you! Rosie thought as she pounced again and again at the toy.

Thoa looked on and laughed at the bouncy little kitten. She grabbed her to give her a kiss.

Rosie felt loved.

"I love you so, so much!" Thi told Rosie.

"Be careful," Tram warned. "Don't get too attached. You know we can't keep her."

"But . . ." Thi started, and then stopped.

Although it would break her heart to give up Rosie, Thi knew it was what she had promised to do.

Thi and her sisters lived in south San Jose, California, in a neighborhood that used to be overrun by stray and feral cats. Strays are used to interacting with humans. Many of them may have been pets at one time. A feral cat is born on the street and usually has a deep fear of humans.

When they were young, Thi, Tram, and

Thoa saved their one-dollar-a-week allowance to buy food for the neighborhood cats. When Thi found kittens, she took care of them—outside at first, bringing them food, water, and warm blankets to sleep on, before her mom started letting her bring their rescues inside. Tram and Thoa joined in, helping Thi care for the cats. When the kittens were old enough, the sisters found the perfect forever home for each one.

Although they worked hard to help the cats, the stray and feral population in their neighborhood continued to skyrocket. The cats they fed went on to have kittens. And then those kittens grew up to have kittens of their own. With their small allowance, there was no way the Bui sisters could care for every single cat there.

When they became teenagers, Thi, Tram,

and Thoa knew they needed more than three dollars a week to help all the cats. So, they got jobs at a local ice-cream store and used that money to help feed the street cats. However, the more money they spent on helping the cats, the more cats there were to help. There had to be something else they could do!

They read about a program that could help control the cat population in their neighborhood: Trap, Neuter, and Release, otherwise known as "TNR." TNR cats are brought to a veterinarian's office, where they are spayed or neutered. The cats are also given some important vaccines to help them stay healthy. After the cats have recovered from surgery, they are released back onto the street with their friends.

This seems like a lot of work to go through,

but the Bui sisters learned that TNR was an effective way to control the number of cats running around on the streets. It meant that fewer cats would eventually end up in animal shelters, too!

By the time Thi, Tram, and Thoa graduated from high school, they had helped more than one hundred feral and stray cats in their neighborhood go through TNR. And every kitten they found during that time was given food and shelter and placed in a forever home. They were truly dedicated to saving cats' lives.

In college, the sisters continued to foster kittens on their own and post about it on social media. People following the sisters on social media loved watching all the kittens being cared for and eventually getting adopted by forever families.

The sisters were doing good work, and people applauded them for it.

"Check this out!" Thoa waved her phone. "I just shot the cutest video of Rosie and Lilo!"

Thoa sat at the kitchen table and showed her family an edited video of Lilo and Rosie cuddling—complete with music.

"That is so sweet!" Thi said.

"I'm crying," Tram said. "Seriously, I think we should post that on YouTube."

"Really?" Thoa asked. "Do you think people will like it? I mean, they like our pics and everything, and our last video got some great comments. But *YouTube*?"

Tram jumped up and took her sister's phone. "Let's find out!"

And with that, she posted the video.

The caption for the video read: *Lilo the Siberian husky is a wonderful surrogate to our new foster, little Rosie. Rosie was really lethargic and unresponsive after the first night. So we decided to let her cuddle extensively with Lilo (the husky). Lilo really surprised us when she went full surrogate mode! Lilo has never had puppies of her own, and never will. But motherhood may just be her calling ☺ Thank you for watching!*

The comments came pouring in:

I don't think I've ever seen anything so beautiful.

It really got me when Rosie put her little head on Lilo's cheek.

And Lilo is so patient, letting Rosie walk all over her <3

See what love can do. This video made me tear up. You all are just awesome.

Love how so many animals will adopt a baby

of another species. They recognize that it's a baby and want to take care of it. <3

The video was a hit. People loved it! Even more, they loved the special bond forming between Rosie and Lilo.

The Bui sisters uploaded more videos of them. With each post, they gained follower after follower who was invested in Rosie and Lilo's relationship. All the while, they continued to care for Rosie, preparing to find her a forever home of her own.

Where are you taking Rosie? Lilo wondered as Thi lifted the sleepy kitten from Lilo's side. Lilo watched as Thi placed Rosie in a carrier. *Is Rosie being taken away from me . . . for good?* Lilo couldn't bear the thought. She whimpered and nudged the outside of the carrier. Inside it,

Rosie, who was now wide awake, looked frightened. Lilo was determined to protect her at all costs!

Little did Lilo know that it was only Rosie's first vet visit.

Thi could tell that Lilo didn't want to let Rosie out of her sight. "You are such a good mama," she told Lilo, giggling. "Don't worry, you're going to come along."

She leashed up Lilo and put her in the car right next to Rosie's carrier.

At the vet, Thi talked about Rosie's rescue. The vet was used to Thi and her sisters bringing in their rescues for checkups. But she wasn't used to Lilo refusing to leave a kitten's side!

Lilo wasn't the only one whose eyes were glued on Rosie.

"You've never seemed so smitten by one of your kittens," the vet told Thi, smiling.

Thi sighed. She secretly imagined being able to keep Rosie forever . . .

Meow! Rosie cried as Thi lifted her. *Where am I? And why am I sitting on this hard, cold table?* This table was certainly not Lilo's cozy fur—it was *freezing* cold and slippery! Rosie's legs slid on the table as a pair of large hands felt her eyes, ears, mouth, and fur. Then the hands gently tapped her tummy and put a piece of icy metal over Rosie's heart.

Her little heart pounded. She was scared. She had to find a way to escape. Rosie wriggled and wriggled, but the hands kept a firm grasp on her.

Just then, Rosie felt Lilo's warm tongue on her paw. *Mama!*

It was as if Lilo was telling her that everything was going to be okay.

And with Lilo by her side, suddenly everything was.

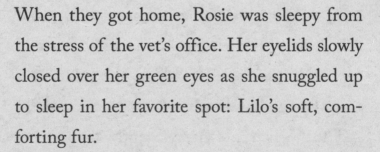

When they got home, Rosie was sleepy from the stress of the vet's office. Her eyelids slowly closed over her green eyes as she snuggled up to sleep in her favorite spot: Lilo's soft, comforting fur.

As Thi watched the two cuddle, tears welled in her eyes.

She knew someone who would be more heartbroken than her when Rosie was adopted: Lilo.

CHAPTER 5
THE UNKNOWN

ONE MORNING, ON A DAY LIKE ANY other, the sisters leashed up huskies Lilo and Finny for a walk.

But when it came time to step outside, Lilo refused to leave.

"Come on, Lilo," Thi urged, giving the leash a little tug. "It's time to go out."

Lilo stayed rooted to the spot, giving

Rosie enough time to run up and nuzzle against her.

Thi laughed. *Of course.* Lilo didn't want to leave Rosie's side!

Lilo licked the top of Rosie's head, and Rosie purred. It was as if Lilo was saying good-bye and telling Rosie that she would be back soon! Rosie meowed. Was she pleading for Lilo not to leave her, even if just for a moment?

"What's up with Lilo this morning?" Tram wondered aloud.

"I think she's anxious about leaving Rosie," Thi said.

"Yeah, but she's been out a ton of times since we've had Rosie. Why is she worried all of a sudden?" Tram asked.

Thi shrugged. "I guess Lilo's just gotten used to having Rosie at her side."

Finny whimpered impatiently at the door.

"Uh, Thi, Finny really needs to go out," Tram said. "Catch up to us, okay?"

Thi nodded and gently tugged on Lilo's leash again. She had to think of another way to get Lilo outside. She took out a treat, dropped Lilo's leash, and walked out the door.

That did the trick. Lilo followed her, and they went for their walk, eventually catching up to Tram and Finny.

Before the next walk, Lilo hesitated again. And the next time, even more strongly.

"Let's go," Thi said. "You have to go outside. Rosie can stay. She has her litter box."

With a litter box, a cat naturally buries their waste, like they would in the wild. Rosie had easily learned how to use one.

But the Bui sisters' dogs didn't use litter boxes, and Lilo had to go outside. Lilo wailed. She simply didn't want to leave Rosie.

Thi sighed. "Lilo, I don't know what I am going to do with you!" Using another treat, she was able to eventually lure Lilo outside again.

When it was time for Lilo's next walk, Thi clipped on her leash.

But once more, Lilo wasn't interested in going out. Instead, she sat down, and Rosie padded up to her and sat down, too. The two were becoming downright inseparable.

Why should I go out without Rosie? Lilo thought. *I don't understand why she has to use that sand-filled box. It's* much *better going outside. Outside is an adventure!* Lilo thought about all the fun things they could do together: pick up sticks, play fetch, sniff and run, and sniff and run more!

Lilo had made up her mind: This time she wouldn't leave without Rosie.

Thi couldn't go through all this fuss every time she needed to take Lilo outside. She needed to figure out how to solve the problem another way.

"Again?" Tram asked Thi when she saw her struggling with Lilo at the door.

Thi nodded.

"Sorry, sis, I'd help you, but I have to get to school," Tram said. "Good luck!"

"Need some help there?" Thoa held out her phone, filming Thi's struggles.

"I don't know what to do with her," Thi told the camera. "I don't think she wants to leave Rosie. Not even for a short walk."

"Awww," Thoa said. "This will make a

great video. I can't wait to post it! Mama Lilo won't leave her baby behind!"

Thi rolled her eyes. Then her mouth fell open in delight. "Maybe I should leash up Rosie, too. That would make for excellent viewing!"

"Hmm . . ." Thoa said. "Interesting. I *have* heard of other cats who are leash trained . . ."

"Yeah, but we've never done it before," Thi said, her mind racing. "And Rosie is still so tiny. How in the world could we find a harness small enough for her?"

"I have an idea." Thoa hurried into the other room.

A few seconds later, she returned holding a harness that they had used for their pet rabbit. "Here, try this."

Thi took the harness from her sister. Amazingly, Rosie slipped into it with ease.

Then Thi clipped a leash onto the harness, and they were ready to go!

"I have *got* to get this on film!" Thoa said. "Finny!" she called. "Time for a walk!"

And with that, the pack set outside for a new adventure.

Lilo and Finny led the way, with Rosie and her short legs trailing behind them.

It was a beautiful day in Northern California. The air was fresh. The sky was blue with puffy white clouds. A few fallen leaves dotted the sidewalk, and Rosie easily trotted over them.

She was a natural on a walk!

Then she slowed down. Thi stopped beside her. Was walking too much for this kitten?

"Wait up, Thoa!" Thi called ahead. "I think Rosie got tired."

Maybe it wasn't a good idea to take her outside after all . . .

But after a few seconds, Rosie started walking again. Perhaps Rosie was just being cautious. After all, it had been only a few months since she had been found on the streets.

Rosie tipped her head back to face the sun, soaking up its delicious warmth. She breathed in the crisp air. She liked this place. Now that she was walking with her new friends, Rosie enjoyed being outdoors: It was a far cry from the hard days and nights spent outside alone and scared.

Oh, look: a bug! Rosie pounced but missed.

This walk was a lot of work! She realized she had fallen behind again, so she padded her little paws as fast as possible on the sun-warmed pavement. It wasn't easy keeping up with Lilo and Finny. They were so fast and full of energy.

Wait for me! she meowed.

As if reading Rosie's mind, Lilo turned around and waited for her to catch up. She even pulled Thoa to a halt.

"Finally!" Thoa joked as Thi and Rosie caught up to them. "Here, take Lilo's leash. Finny has a ton of energy, so I'm going to run ahead with her."

Thi took Lilo's leash as Lilo nudged Rosie with her nose. When Lilo stopped to go potty, so did Rosie! Thi couldn't believe it: a kitten who goes to the bathroom outside and not in a litter box!

Just then, another dog who was off leash approached. Lilo started to bark.

"Easy, girl," Thi said, trying to calm Lilo down. She knew that Lilo still had anxiety around other dogs, and what made it worse was that this dog wasn't on a leash. He was alone.

Frantically, Thi looked around for the dog's owner.

The dog moved closer, and Lilo began to shake and growl.

"Hello! Anyone with this dog?" Thi shouted, holding Lilo back while trying to remain calm.

Rosie nuzzled up against Lilo, and just like that, Lilo began to relax a bit.

Thi was amazed: *Was Rosie good for Lilo's fear and anxiety issues?*

Was it possible that Rosie could help Lilo just as much as Lilo was helping Rosie?

Thankfully, the other dog's owner jogged

up to join them. "Sorry about that," the young woman said, wiping sweat from her forehead. "We were out for a run, and she just ran ahead of me." She quickly clipped a leash on her dog's collar and speed-walked away down the street.

Thi took a nice deep breath. "I think we've had enough excitement for one day, girls. Let's head home!"

"Good girl," Thi told Rosie when they finally returned home from their walk. She gave their amazing pets treats for being so well-behaved on their first outdoor adventure together.

After all that activity, Rosie was pooped. She curled up next to Lilo for a long nap.

When it came time for the next walk, Rosie was ready to go! The walks with her friends continued. Each walk stretched longer and longer. And with each one, Rosie mimicked the dogs more and more. She even started walking with her tail up—and wagging!

One day while Thi was bottle-feeding Rosie, she noticed a small white speck on Rosie's gums.

"What do we have here, Rosie?" Thi asked. "Could this be your premolars growing in?"

Given Rosie's age, Thi knew this was a very real possibility, which meant it was time to start weaning Rosie from the bottle and introducing her to solid food.

Thi gently pried open Rosie's mouth. "Yep, suspicion confirmed," she said. "I think it's time we try some solid food!"

It is best to start a kitten off with wet food. Like with kitten milk, Thi knew it was important to get food specially made for growing kittens. In the past, Thi and her sisters had difficulty introducing wet food to the foster kittens. They usually had to slowly introduce the food or mix it with formula in a bowl. And some kittens really wanted to stick with formula. In those instances, the sisters decided it wouldn't harm the kittens if they stayed on the bottle for a few weeks longer. They knew it was important to listen to each kitten's specific needs. But what would Rosie think?

Thi held out her finger with some food on it. "Okay, let's see how you do."

Rosie immediately lapped up the food.

Thi smiled. "Wow, girl, you are all in!"

Just like with everything else in her life so far, Rosie proved she was up for the challenge.

"I love you so much, Rosie." Thi scooped her up to cuddle. "You are one special kitten."

Thi set a bowl of kitten food down next to Lilo's bowl of kibble. When Lilo ate, so did Rosie.

Yummy, yum, yum! Rosie thought. *This is so tasty!* Rosie finished her food and scampered across the room. Then she jumped on Lilo's back. *Now I eat the same as you, Lilo! Wanna play?*

But Lilo's tummy was full and all she wanted to do was nap.

Come on, Lilo! Jump! Run! Lilo didn't react. She was sound asleep.

So, Rosie ran over to Thi and nuzzled her legs. And guess what?

Thi brought out Rosie's favorite toy.

Wheeee! It's playtime!

Although Rosie loved her wet food, Thi still weighed her each day to make sure she was getting enough nutrients. If she wasn't gaining enough weight, then Thi had to give Rosie a bottle, too.

The good news was that Rosie was growing just as she should. The not-so-good news? The time was fast-approaching when Thi would give Rosie up for adoption. That was *always* what she and her sisters had done: Because they rescued kittens so often, there was no way they could keep them. Besides, the Bui family already had pets at home. Apart from Lilo and Finny, they still had the two cats Thi had rescued in middle school, plus some fish and two rabbits!

Thoa continued to post pictures of Lilo and Rosie on social media, and the number of followers kept increasing. Their followers now included people from all over the world. Everyone agreed that Lilo and Rosie were so incredibly cute together! One of their followers on Instagram wrote: *I just love unusual animal friendships, one of my most favorite things ever! I hope you keep Rosie. I think Lilo and Rosie would be heartbroken if you didn't. Best wishes from the U.K.*

As the bond between Lilo and Rosie strengthened, so did the bond between Rosie and the Bui sisters. They took Rosie out on daily walks with the pack, played with her, and even sometimes let Rosie cuddle up with them in their beds.

One morning, Thi woke up to Rosie snuggling next to her. "Good morning, little one," Thi said, stretching. She grabbed her phone to check their social media accounts and scrolled through the comments as Rosie crawled across her.

Then Thi checked her calendar to see what was happening for the day.

She sat up with a start, sending Rosie tumbling onto the soft blanket.

Today, Rosie was eight weeks old.

Which meant today was also the day they had to start to find Rosie her forever home.

"Oh no," Thi cried out with a heavy heart.

Tram and Thoa came charging into her bedroom.

"Is everything okay?" a worried Thoa asked.

"Check out the date." Thi held out her phone. There in red on her calendar was a reminder to begin Rosie's adoption process. "I . . . I want to keep her," Thi admitted to her sisters.

"So do I," Tram confessed, sitting on the edge of the bed and petting Rosie.

"But you know our rule," Thoa chimed in,

folding her arms across her chest. "We nurse them back to health and then we find them a good home. It's what we've always done."

Thi hung her head. "You're right." Although inside she wished this wasn't the case.

Lilo came into the room to check out all the commotion. As soon as Rosie saw her, she hopped off Thi's bed to give Lilo some morning kisses. When Thi and her sisters looked at Rosie and Lilo being so loving with each other, their hearts broke even more at the thought of Rosie going. The bond between dog and kitten was so powerful. How could they ever separate the two?

But rules are rules.

Right?

CHAPTER 6
NEVER SAY GOODBYE

"I DON'T KNOW," THOA SAID, shaking her head. "I love Rosie just as much as everyone else, but we have a lot on our plate these days."

Thi knew Thoa was right. After people learned about Rosie from social media, the sisters were getting more calls than ever about rescuing neonatal kittens. And even though they loved their work, they were exhausted. Between school and jobs and the round-the-clock bottle feedings and getting all the kittens adopted, it was a lot. Taking on more wasn't an option. But still . . .

Thi watched Rosie and Lilo playing. Rosie was truly becoming an honorary husky, and Lilo had been so happy, and way less anxious, ever since Rosie arrived—she seemed to be enjoying her role as her mother. It broke Thi's heart that they wouldn't be able to keep Rosie.

Poor Lilo would be devastated.

"Let's put our feelings aside for a minute," Thi said. "Adopting Rosie out will really crush Lilo. I've noticed a real change in her since Rosie came into our lives."

Tram and Thoa nodded.

"Well, what's one more pet?" Thoa suggested with a slight smile.

"Agreed!" Tram said.

Thi let out a happy laugh, tears of joy forming in her eyes. She knelt down and lovingly wrapped Rosie in a warm embrace. "Yay! Rosie, girl, you are officially part of the Bui pack!"

"Road trip!" Tram shouted excitedly.

"Yes—to celebrate!" Thoa added merrily.

"Let's get Miko to come, too!" Tram said. Miko was Lilo's and Finny's brother, and he lived with Tram's friend.

It would be their first road trip as a forever family. Rosie was there to stay.

Thi put Rosie in the back seat of the car, right next to Lilo. *Meow! I don't like it in here!* Rosie complained. *It's stuffy and hot. I want out.* Rosie started pawing at the door. No matter what anyone did to try to calm her down, Rosie was desperate to get out of the car. Even Lilo's kisses were of no comfort. *Get me out of here! Help! I don't want to go to the vet!*

"What's up with Rosie?" Tram asked. "She's always so eager to come along with us."

Thi didn't understand Rosie's protests, either. But after a moment, Thi understood why Rosie was scratching at the door. "You know, the last time Rosie was in the car was on the way to the vet," Thi reasoned. "And before that, it was when I brought her in from off the street."

"That's a good point," Thoa said. "Rosie doesn't have good memories linked with cars."

Tram hated seeing little Rosie so upset. "So should we head back home?" she asked.

Thi shook her head. "Let's just drive a little while longer and stop at the park. I think it's best to get Rosie used to the car bit by bit."

"Yeah," Tram agreed. "Because we love our family road trips!"

This is much better, Rosie thought, sniffing the fresh air. *Much better than that awful car! Come on, guys, let's have some fun!* And with her tail held high, Rosie led the way through the park.

Rosie pulled at her leash, making Thi walk faster through a grassy field.

I like it here! Rosie thought. *Lilo, catch up to me!*

Soon, Rosie forgot all about the car.

After playing, the pack headed back to the car. Lilo, Finny, and Miko jumped in, but not Rosie.

"Come on, Rosie, the car isn't that bad," Thi

said. "This time it took us somewhere fun."

But Rosie wasn't budging.

Thi picked her up and put her down in the back seat next to Lilo.

It's okay, Rosie. Lilo nuzzled up close to Rosie and kissed her. *I know how you're feeling, like your heart is beating fast and you have a funny feeling in your tummy. But the car is fun, you'll see. It takes us to lots of great places, like the mountains and the beach and the lake. Hey, I bet you're really going to like kayaking! You just have to take some time to get used to the car.*

Each week, Thi took Rosie for rides in the car. With each ride, Rosie became more and more comfortable.

"Okay, I think we are ready for a longer road trip," Thi announced one morning.

"Yes!" Tram agreed. "Where to this time?"

"Los Angeles!" Thi suggested.

"That's over a five-hour ride," Thoa pointed out. "Do you think Rosic is up for it?"

Thi nodded. "I do!"

The sisters packed their bags—with tons of homemade treats—and headed to the car.

Rosie went in without a struggle.

"And we're off!" Thi said as she started the engine and turned on the radio.

As she drove, she kept an eye on Rosie through the rearview mirror.

Rosie and Lilo were behaving just like mischievous siblings! Lilo nibbled on Rosie's paws, and Rosie swatted Lilo in the eye and then playfully chomped at her ear!

"Behave, you two!" an amused Thi called from the driver's seat.

Meow! Meow! Rosie was having too much fun. She stared at Thi with her big green eyes.

"Fine," Thi said with a laugh. "Keep playing. As long as nobody gets hurt!"

Although the car trip to LA was long, the pack had a blast once they arrived. They hiked some nature trails and walked along streets in the city. And Rosie had fun getting to explore another new place with the pack!

One day, the Bui sisters took Rosie to the local park. The sun was low in the sky, and the air was heavy with rain clouds. Rosie sniffed the grass as she walked on her leash next to Lilo and Finny.

The two dogs were used to roaming free in

the park, so Tram and Thoa let go of their leashes. They ran about, smelling trees, going potty, and having fun, racing with their tongues hanging out. But Rosie wasn't enjoying herself fully: She wanted to run free with the pack, too.

Thi felt that Rosie was anxious. "Do you want to run?" she asked Rosie, who was gently pulling on her leash. Then Rosie shook her body—not in a scared way, but in a way that said she clearly wanted off her leash.

"Hmm," Thi said. "What do you think about me letting Rosie off her leash?"

"I don't know," Thoa said. "I'm afraid she might run off. Isn't that typical cat instinct?"

Tram grinned. "Rosie isn't your typical cat. She's part of the pack!"

Thoa and Thi nodded. Then, holding her breath, Thi took a chance. She dropped the leash, and Rosie ran off—to catch up with Lilo and Finny and join in on their fun!

Wheeee! This is the life. Running free, free, free! Rosie scampered with Lilo and Finny, the warm wind rustling her fur. *Wait for me!* Rosie was happy when Lilo turned around. Her eyes were wide. *Yes, I'm running free just like you!* And when Rosie passed Lilo, Lilo raced to catch up.

What a perfect day!

After running around for a while, Lilo, Finny, and Rosie were exhausted. The sisters leashed the animals back up and headed to the car.

"Excuse me." A young woman walking an adorable cocker spaniel stopped them.

Thi held on tightly to Lilo's leash. "Yes?" she said.

"Isn't that Lilo and Rosie? I follow them on Instagram!" the woman gushed. She practically had hearts in her eyes as she looked at them. "They are even cuter in person!"

"This is them!" Thi said, shocked that someone actually recognized them in the real world. "And I'm . . ." but she didn't get to finish her sentence as the woman snapped a picture and headed off.

"Rosie and Lilo are stars," Tram said with a chuckle.

"Without them, I guess we're just regular people!" Thi told her sisters.

Tram and Thoa laughed. Rosie and Lilo were truly becoming real-life celebrities!

After one particularly long walk, Thoa uploaded a video to YouTube with a caption:

Rosie the kitten walking on leash with her husky pack! We trekked about 3 miles (1 hour) through the park. She is about 4 months old here! Thank you for watching!

Immediately, the comments for the video came pouring in:

I simply cannot express how I feel about this cute family.

She has to walk fast with her little legs if she wants to stay in the pack. So funny, I love watching her.

Whatever Rosie believes she is—cat or dog— she's loved and happy. With all those buddy-dogs, it's no surprise.

Did Rosie believe she was a dog? She still used her litter box inside, and she still ate cat food. Either way, Rosie was a phenomenon, and her fame was only beginning to blossom.

CHAPTER 7
A STAR IS BORN

"OH MY GOSH, I CAN'T BELIEVE this!" Thi shouted one morning as she scrolled through the comments on a Lilo and Rosie video that Thoa had recently uploaded to YouTube.

"Is everything okay?" Thoa asked, racing into her bedroom, joined shortly by Tram.

Thi bolted up in bed and nodded. "You are

not going to believe this. We got a message from a producer from National Geographic's *Unlikely Animal Friends* show."

Thi stood on her bed and began to jump up and down.

"And?!" Tram asked impatiently, too excited to wait on details.

"This producer wants to speak with us about possibly doing a show on Rosie and Lilo!"

"Wait, what exactly is this show?" Thoa asked.

Thi plopped down on her bed and began to explain. "This is what it says: '*Unlikely Animal Friends* features heartwarming stories of unbreakable bonds formed between two animals of a different species, or an animal and a human friend,'" she read from her phone.

"Wow," Thoa said. "I can't believe our story

has traveled so far. I mean, we have a *producer* from National Geographic interested in featuring our pack. This is huge!"

"It is . . ." Thi agreed, heart racing. "Let's set up a call!"

Thi, Thoa, and Tram sat around the kitchen table staring nervously at the phone in front of them.

"When do you think the call will come in?" Tram asked.

Thoa checked the time. "We have a few minutes. Relax." But Thoa was just as nervous and excited as her sisters.

Finally, the phone rang. The sisters jumped at the sound.

Thi eagerly snatched up the phone and answered. "Hello, this is Thi."

"Hello," the producer said. "Are your sisters there with you?"

"We are," Thoa and Tram chimed in.

The producer told them that Lilo and Rosie's story had captured her heart and that she wanted to pitch their story to the executives at National Geographic. If it went well, they'd get filmed for TV! Who ever thought Lilo and Rosie would go from phone screens to TV screens?

Thi pumped her fist with excitement. "That sounds great," she told the producer.

"But before I pitch this story, I want you all to think carefully if this is okay with you," the producer said. "Take some time to think about it. Because once I pitch it and it's accepted, everything's a go."

"We will think about it, and thank you," Thi said. "We'll get back to you soon."

As soon as Thi hung up the phone, she and her sisters danced around yelling with joy.

"This is so cool."

"We are going to be famous!"

"The world is going to know their names!"

"Not to be a downer," Thoa said, "but how do you think they'll react to being filmed, especially Lilo?"

"Well, there won't be any other dogs around to risk upsetting her," Tram said.

"True . . ." Thi nodded. "But what if Rosie just hides under my bed the entire time?"

"Come on, has Rosie *ever* done that?" Tram asked teasingly.

"No," Thi said with a laugh. "I guess now *I'm* being the protective mama."

"The show *will* bring a lot of exposure to our family," Thoa pointed out. "Much more than my little videos. Do you think *we* can handle it? All the attention?"

"Yes!" Thi and Tram said at the same time.

"Especially if our message about the importance of rescuing cats reaches more people," Thi said with a firm nod. If they could inspire kindness toward cats, Thi would be overjoyed.

"Then it's a go," Thoa agreed.

Thi called the producer back and told her that this was an opportunity they couldn't pass up. The producer was excited and said she'd pitch the story and let them know the outcome.

A few long weeks later, the call finally came: their story was "green-lit," which meant that filming was on! The shoot was scheduled for August 6, 2015.

"This is so exciting!" Thi marked the date of the filming on her phone calendar.

"Yes," Thoa agreed. "But I'm nervous. I mean the only filming we've done so far has been on our phones and GoPros. Now we'll have an actual film crew with an actual camera!"

"It's a bummer we can't tell any of our friends what's happening," Tram said. They promised the producer they would keep Lilo and Rosie's episode super top secret before it aired on TV.

Thi nodded. "Yup, but everyone will be so excited when they finally see the episode!"

Thi picked up Rosie and squeezed her. "You are going to be famous!"

Lilo barked, and the sisters laughed.

"Yes, you too, Lilo!" Thi said.

Buuuuzzzzz! Sleepily, Thi shut off her alarm. She looked at her phone: It was only 6:30 a.m. Why was her alarm already going off? She stretched and rolled over. Suddenly, she shot up. Today was the day the filming began! She quickly got dressed and met her sisters in the living room.

"Ready?" Thi asked with a nervous smile.

Thoa and Tram nodded. They'd leashed up Lilo and Finny. They were going to take the dogs out for an early run. Hopefully, with all that exercise and from releasing so much energy, they'd be nice and calm when the film crew finally arrived in less than two hours.

Thi laced up her sneakers and grabbed Lilo's leash. Lilo sat down.

"Come, on, Lilo," Thi said, "this is not the time to be stubborn."

But Lilo saw that Rosie wasn't leashed,

and she didn't want to go out without her.

"We can't take Rosie out with us," Thoa tried to explain. "We need to run this morning."

"And we're going to run fast," Tram added. "Rosie's little legs won't be able to keep up!"

Thi said goodbye to Rosie, grabbed a treat, and finally lured Lilo outside.

The sun had just risen, and a layer of haze masked the sky. It felt good to be outside. Thi took in deep breaths as she and Lilo settled into a comfortable running pace.

This run is just as much for me as it is for Lilo, Thi thought as she tried to shake off her nerves. It was going to be a long day: The filming was set to take place over twelve hours!

As soon as they returned home, Lilo went to find Rosie, who was comfortably curled up on Lilo's bed as if waiting for her to return!

Finny lapped up water and Thi, Thoa, and Tram each went to shower and change into nice outfits.

At eight o'clock, the doorbell rang.

"I got it!" Tram called out. "Good morning," she said cheerfully as she opened the door.

The producer handed her a box of doughnuts. "I brought you an early morning present."

"Thank you!" Tram didn't know about her sisters, but she was hungry after their run.

By 8:30 a.m., three producers, a camera guy, and a sound guy had all crowded into their house. Cables, cords, and cameras were everywhere. There was so much equipment!

"Okay, time to get you all ready," the sound guy said.

The sisters looked at one another: They thought they were all ready to go.

Rosie the cat was rescued from the streets when she was just a kitten. She was very small and hungry when the Bui sisters found her. They nursed Rosie back to health by bottle-feeding her and making sure she got plenty of rest.

Rosie became fast friends with the Bui sisters' huskies, Lilo and Finny, and their friend Miko.

The Bui sisters call the dogs their "pack." Rosie quickly became part of the pack, too!

The more time Rosie spent with the dogs, the more Rosie started acting like a dog herself!

Rosie loves wearing a leash and going on long walks with her dog siblings.

And just like a dog, she loves learning new tricks—like giving high fives!

Rosie loves all the dogs, but Lilo is her best friend. When Rosie was still a kitten, Lilo acted like her mother and helped the Bui sisters take good care of Rosie.

The two share a very special bond.

From the beginning, Rosie and Lilo have done everything together, like taking catnaps . . .

. . . and having story time before bed!

Lilo helped Rosie become a brave adventure cat! These days, Rosie enjoys hiking in the great outdoors, exploring the tall grass, and sniffing everything in sight.

Rosie isn't as fond of snowy adventures, though . . . BRRR! It's a good thing she always has Lilo to keep her warm.

Rosie and Lilo even love to go out on the water! They wear special life jackets when they go kayaking or paddleboarding with their humans.

Rosie feels so lucky to have found a loving family and be part of the pack—and Lilo wouldn't have it any other way.

What else was there to do?

The producer noticed their puzzled looks. "You each have to be fitted for a microphone so we can easily pick up what you say."

Everyone nodded: Now it made sense. Of course, the sisters would be in the show, too!

The sound guy handed each sister a box and instructed them how to clip it on and run its wire up below their chins, where it was taped down and hidden from view of the cameras.

"Perfect!" the sound guy said when they were finished. "Now we are ready to go!"

"What do you want us to do?" Thi asked.

"We want to film you having a typical day with Rosie and Lilo," the producer explained. "Try to relax and ignore that we're even here. We want this to look as natural as possible."

Thi went into the kitchen and set out the food for Lilo and Rosie. One of the camera guys knelt and placed his camera down on the floor to get a good close-up shot of Lilo chowing down. And then he filmed Rosie lapping up her wet food.

"So, can you tell us about rescuing Rosie?" the producer asked Thi during an "On the Fly," or OTF, interview.

Thi stared right into the camera and started to explain.

But then the camera guy put his camera down.

"Sorry . . ." Thi said. "What did I do? Did I do something wrong?"

"Try not to stare directly into the camera when you're speaking. It'll feel more natural," the producer shared in a friendly way.

Thi nodded and began to answer the interview question again, pretending like the camera wasn't even there. Whenever she or her sisters stumbled over their words a bit, the crew kindly let them have a do-over.

"We're going to head to the park," Thi said when she noticed Lilo and Rosie were getting restless. They weren't used to bright lights and equipment. "Is that okay?" she asked the producer.

"Of course! As we said, we want to film a typical day here!"

Thi leashed up Lilo and Rosie, and Tram leashed up Finny. It was a weird feeling having a film crew following them down the street, but they tried to remain as natural as they could.

As soon as they got to the park, a crowd had gathered, curious to see what was going on.

Although they couldn't reveal exactly what they were filming, the crew interviewed a few of the bystanders about what they thought about Rosie and Lilo.

"Ha!" Tram pointed at Lilo lounging in the grass. "She is posing for a glamour shot!"

One of the cameramen bent down to capture Lilo looking like a professional model.

Of course, Rosie wanted in on the action, too. She strutted by as the cameras were filming.

Let me off leash! Rosie thought as she tumbled through the grass. *I want to show what I can do!* As if reading her mind, Thi unclasped Rosie's leash from the harness.

I'm free! Rosie ran so fast that the man holding the camera had a hard time keeping up with her. *Watch this.* Rosie leaped up. Then she caught a bug. Next, she stopped for a moment to sniff a tall blade of grass. *How do I look?* Rosie groomed her fur, and then she was off again.

Catch me if you can! And with that, Rosie scampered up the trunk of a tree.

Lilo barked until she came back down to safety on the grass below.

After a lunch break, the sit-down interview started. Thoa sat in front of a set of stage lights, and a makeup artist from the crew powdered her face with a round brush. She knew that the producer had a long list of questions for her, so she closed her eyes for a moment and mentally prepared.

It was time. The cameras turned on, and the sit-down interview began.

"When Lilo and Rosie are together," Thoa

said as the cameras rolled, "they live in this bubble. From her relationship with Lilo, she has grown into this catlike dog. She walks on a leash and plays very roughly with the dogs."

"Great, but can you repeat that answer?" the producer asked.

"Did I say something wrong?" Thoa wondered aloud.

The producer shook his head. "It was perfect. We just want to shoot from a different angle now. It's a standard thing we do for TV. It lets us show you from a few different sides."

Thoa answered that question again and the other questions, too, with all the enthusiasm she could muster. She was so excited that this show would bring even more attention to Rosie and Lilo and their remarkable friendship. Throughout it all, the big smile never left Thoa's face.

"That was great, Thoa," the producer said when they shot all the footage they'd need.

Off to the side, Thi's heart raced. She knew where they were going next: to the vet's office, where Rosie was scheduled for an appointment. Rosie would not be happy—not one bit!

"Rosie absolutely hates vet visits," Thoa shared with the crew, voicing Thi's concern.

Rosie was due to get her rabies shot. Rabies is a disease that can be found in wild animals such as raccoons and is passed on through saliva. Being bitten by an animal infected by rabies is the most common way of getting infected. If a cat becomes infected, it makes them very sick, and can be deadly. Getting a rabies shot is a necessity to protect pets against rabies.

The entire crew came along to the vet's office. Rosie immediately knew where she was.

Nervously, she crept down and slinked along the waiting room floor. Was there any way out? Maybe she could hide? Rosie and Lilo sat together on a bench, waiting to be called in.

The vet had cleared her schedule so there would be no other animals there to make Lilo anxious during the shoot. Still, the small office felt cramped with the cameramen, sound guy, and producer.

At last, the vet was camera-ready, and Thi carried a shaking Rosie into the chilly examination room, Lilo by her side. With Rosie on the steel table, the camera rolled.

"It is adorable how much they love each other," Rosie's vet said, "as well as that Lilo is Rosie's rock in a sense, and that they just do great together."

And Lilo was certainly Rosie's rock again as the vet injected the shot into Rosie's leg.

Ouch! With Lilo's support, Rosie had been able to face her fears.

After it was done, Lilo smothered her with big wet kisses.

Later that night, the Bui sisters returned home, weary and sleepy. Rosie and Lilo were sound asleep within seconds of coming home. They were all so tired that they could hardly stand. The day of filming had been a lot more work than they'd thought.

It was worth it, though.

It was only a matter of time before many people would learn about the amazing story of the love shared between Rosie and Lilo.

CHAPTER 8
THIS CAT WAS MADE FOR HIKING

"THE FILMING WAS SO MUCH FUN!" Thoa said a few days later, "but I'm still exhausted!"

Thi chuckled. "So am I," she agreed. "But I can't wait until even more people find out about Lilo and Rosie's special bond."

"Same," Tram added.

"This might sound strange, but maybe

people will learn how to get along better by watching Rosie and Lilo," Thi said. "I mean, if two animals who are so different can love and support each other, why can't the same be true of *people* who are different from one another?"

"Very true," Thoa said. "So, where's our next adventure? We need to keep filming and posting videos to spread Rosie and Lilo's message."

"Hiking!" Tram suggested. And Thi and Thoa agreed.

Believe it or not, taking cats on hikes is a popular thing to do in the summertime. But before taking a cat on a hike, preparations must be made. Rosie had already checked many of the boxes: She was used to car rides now and was comfortable walking with a leash and harness. The Bui sisters knew to bring along supplies, such as water, food, and a cat backpack in case Rosie got tired from all that walking. In addition, they made sure Rosie, as well as the dogs, were protected from ticks and other tiny critters who might try to hitch a ride on their fur. They also researched which trail would be best for a cat. A quiet trail is ideal, since loud sudden noises can easily startle a cat. The trail needs to allow cats on it, too.

Once the sisters felt they were prepared, they ventured out on a short hike with Rosie and the pack. Thi carried the backpack so Rosie could be carried if she stopped wanting to walk.

"I'll walk with Rosie," Thi said, "and you go ahead with Lilo and Finny." The sisters always made sure that each pet had at least one handler in case anything went wrong. It wasn't safe to let the animals wander around a trail on their own.

As Rosie wandered along, she took time to smell the dewy blades of grass and the large deep-purple flowers. *It's nice to slow down and enjoy nature*, Thi thought as she watched Rosie sniffing pebbles, nudging tree branches, and pawing at soft moss growing on the base of trees.

"Thoa, Tram, check this out!" Thi called.

They walked back to Rosie, who stood nose to nose with a little green salamander.

"Looks like Rosie made a new friend," Tram said with a laugh.

Lilo whimpered at the sight.

"Don't worry," Thoa said, petting her. "Rosie still loves you."

For the rest of the hike, Lilo didn't let Rosie out of view.

But when they came to a waterfall, Lilo ran right through it, leaving Rosie behind.

Rosie shivered, frozen in place as she eyed the rushing sheet of water.

"It's okay, Rosie," Thi said. "It's just water."

Lilo tried showing Rosie to be brave since a lot of cats are frightened of water.

Rosie sniffed the air and followed in Lilo's path, letting the water wash over her!

Later that week, the Bui sisters and their pack went for a hike in the Northern Californian redwood forest. Redwoods are magnificent giant trees that grow to three hundred feet or more! Although the huge redwood trees soared high above Rosie, she padded along with the pack. Then they came across a dog. Thi picked up Rosie, unsure as to what would happen. But she sensed the dog was friendly and lowered Rosie slowly toward him.

Rosie stuck out her furry white paw, as if to say hello, and patted the dog on his nose!

The dog stood there, slightly confused, but he seemed to enjoy meeting Rosie, too!

One of the sisters' favorite hikes with Rosie and the pack was to Uvas Canyon County Park in Morgan Hill, California. The Uvas Canyon Waterfall Loop is a lovely hike over rolling hills, babbling creeks, and cascading waterfalls. Rosie sniffed the foliage as she trekked after Lilo, Finny, and their mix-breed cousin, DJ. She pranced over the twigs, branches, and leaves that crunched beneath her paws. Every so often, she would stop to sniff out something new—everything smelled delicious.

As the sun's rays streamed down between the branches, Rosie scrambled up a tree trunk.

Lilo barked as if to say: "Be careful!"

"Check out Rosie," Tram said after Rosie scampered back down and ran after Lilo.

Tram and her sisters sped to catch up to them.

Lilo had already run ahead, but Rosie stopped short.

"Why did you stop?" Thoa asked. "Is there something frightening you?"

Thi walked ahead and saw a dip in the ground—a shallow ravine. The only way across it was over a narrow wooden plank. But Rosie wasn't scared. She was just checking out the situation. Then she crossed to the other side, where Lilo stood patiently waiting for her.

The sisters laughed. "That's the last time I'll doubt Rosie," Thoa said.

"She faces every challenge head-on!" Thi agreed.

But after walking for a few more minutes, Rosie couldn't fight her exhaustion.

Thi picked her up and put her gently in her backpack for a well-deserved rest.

Another favorite place to hike was Anderson Lake County Park in Morgan Hill, California, with its gorgeous trails, sprawling man-made lake, and fast-flowing streams. This was the pack's first visit to the park, and they were uncertain of what to expect.

Where did all these people come from? Rosie wondered as they passed tons of people walking, jogging, and biking. *I like hiking in quiet with just the pack and me.* Rosie trembled.

"It seems calmer here, and I don't see anyone else around," Thi said when they came upon a narrow dirt trail. She let the dogs off leash and pulled Rosie from her backpack to roam free on the path.

"I think this path leads to the lake," Tram said, reading a map.

"Um, I think this trail is taking us back home, not to the lake," Thoa said after they walked for a while under the cool shade of the trees.

As they turned around, a huge wild turkey appeared on the path!

Quickly, the sisters leashed up the dogs and grabbed Rosie.

Lilo barked and Rosie squirmed in Thi's arms.

"Easy there," Thi said, trying to calm Rosie down.

"Do you think she doesn't like birds?" Tram asked. "I mean, cats and birds don't mix."

Just then, the turkey flapped their wings and flew up into a tree.

"Oh, look!" Tram pointed up at the tree. "Look how many turkeys are perched up there!" Five turkey were nestled in the tree's branches.

"As long as they stay out of our way, I'm happy," Thoa said.

"Same," Thi said. "Hey, why don't we let the pack have fun in that field over there?"

The group headed over to the grassy area that Thi had pointed out, where the dogs frolicked in the tall grass. Rosie did what she did best: sniffed the flowers with curiosity.

"It's getting pretty hot out here," Thoa said after a while. "Even though we're all well hydrated, I don't think it's really safe for any of us to be outside in this heat for much longer."

Tram and Thi agreed, so they decided to skip the lake and take the path back to the car.

Suddenly, a large animal blocked their way!

It looked a lot like a pig, only larger—a *lot* larger.

"Oh my gosh," Tram said. "Look at that thing. It's at least five feet tall!"

"That's a bit of an exaggeration," Thoa said with a nervous laugh, "but it is pretty big."

"And it's headed right toward us," Thi said. Her heart began to race as the large animal, who was covered with dark bristly hair, started to paw the ground and grunt, their ears wiggling.

"That's a wild boar, and they don't look too friendly," Thoa said.

"What should we do?" a panicked Tram asked. "Stay still? Turn and run?"

"I wouldn't run," Thoa said, petting Lilo to keep her from charging the boar.

Lilo calmly stepped in front of Rosie as if trying to protect her from the boar.

And then, just like that, the boar took one last look at them and lumbered off the path.

Phew!

Back in their car, the sisters posted a new video of Rosie and the pack's hiking adventure on YouTube. Viewers were touched by how much love was visible between Rosie and Lilo.

Seeing animals from two different species getting along so well was inspiring!

Rosie and Lilo's story, and message of togetherness, was resonating around the world.

CHAPTER 9
SOMETIMES LIFE ISN'T SO FUN

ROSIE WAS SET TO BE SPAYED IN THE morning, and Thi paced back and forth. She was nervous about how Rosie would get through the procedure.

"It's going to be okay," Thoa said, resting her hand on her sister's shoulder and forcing her to stay still for a moment. "Rosie will get through the surgery just fine."

"Thoa's right," Tram added. "There's nothing to be worried about. We've had tons of cats— ours and our fosters—spayed and neutered, and they've all come through with flying colors."

"I know she'll be fine, but I'm still nervous," Thi said. "And look at her walking back and forth to the kitchen. She must be so hungry and thirsty." But Thi knew she had to follow all the vet's instructions leading up to the surgery, and one of them was no food or water the night before.

It's okay, Rosie. Lilo nuzzled up to Rosie, trying to get her to stop pacing like Thi was.

I remember being hungry before my surgery, too. Don't worry, you can eat tomorrow.

Rosie finally settled down, and Lilo kissed her on the nose.

The surgery will make you hazy afterward, but you'll feel better fast. I promise.

And with that, Rosie and Lilo fell asleep for the night.

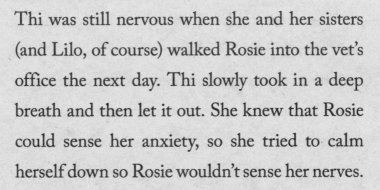

Thi was still nervous when she and her sisters (and Lilo, of course) walked Rosie into the vet's office the next day. Thi slowly took in a deep breath and then let it out. She knew that Rosie could sense her anxiety, so she tried to calm herself down so Rosie wouldn't sense her nerves.

Lilo, on the other hand, was doing a good job of keeping Rosie calm, covering her with big sloppy kisses. When the vet came out to take Rosie into the surgery room, Lilo whimpered.

"It's okay, girl," Thi said. "Rosie will be just fine."

Thi, Tram, and Thoa paced in the waiting room, eager for Rosie's surgery to finish. Lilo's eyes remained fixed on the door where Rosie had last passed through with the nice vet.

"Come on," Thoa said, "we all have to relax."

"Thoa's right," Tram said. "And it's silly to wait here all day. The vet said she'd call us when Rosie was done. Ice cream, anyone?"

"Yes!" Thi said.

The sisters left the office and drove to downtown San Jose, which they like to say is "a big city with a small-town feel." After parking, they walked with Lilo along Santana Row, a street filled with cute shops and stores.

"Hey, Lilo, where's Rosie?" asked a woman passing by.

Thi would never get used to people

recognizing them on the streets from their social media posts. "Um, she's at the vet," Thi said, not wanting to give more information than they'd posted online earlier.

"Hope she's okay," the woman said. "I just love seeing those two together!"

"She'll be up and out in no time," Thoa said with a smile.

When they reached one of their favorite ice-cream shops, Thoa and Tram offered to go inside and order while Thi and Lilo sat on the grass outside. They emerged moments later with one cookie dough with pretzels, cookie dough in a waffle cone, and roasted banana.

And a bowl with one scoop of plain vanilla ice cream.

Lilo looked anxious, likely worrying about Rosie. But she seemed relieved and happy when Tram set the bowl of vanilla ice cream down in front of her. It was gone in seconds!

When the call came from the vet, Thi quickly but carefully drove everyone back to the office. Just as they arrived, the vet was leading Rosie out of the surgery room and down a hall.

"Oh. My. Goodness." Thi covered her mouth, trying not to giggle.

There was Rosie, with a plastic cone in the shape of a lion's mane around her head.

"She is so cute!" Tram said. "But probably in a lot of pain, so we really shouldn't laugh."

"Sorry, I couldn't help it. I haven't seen anything so adorable in all my life!"

"Come on, Rosie," Thoa said, gently lifting her. "Time to go home and rest."

I hear someone calling my name, but I can't see a thing, and what in the world is around my neck?

Rosie bumped into a wall and bounced. Then she bumped into another wall and bounced again. *I have to get this thing off me!* But no matter how much she tried, it stayed put, hindering her movements. *Hey, wall, watch out: You just hit me!* Rosie thought as she continued to struggle walking down the hallway. *All I want right now is for this thing to be OFF!*

"I have to rescue her," Thi said after watching Rosie bump into the wall one too many times.

She followed Rosie and picked her up. Lilo wanted to help, too, by giving Rosie kisses, but Thi didn't want Lilo to get too close to Rosie's stitches just in case.

Right after the surgery, Rosie was given an injection to ease her pain, but the sisters made sure to also have pain medication at home in case Rosie was still uncomfortable. It is hard to tell if a cat is in pain, but Thi, Thoa, and Tram were so in tune with Rosie that they knew they would be able to pick up the signs. They also knew to keep an eye on Rosie's stitches. They watched the area for any redness or swelling. If there was any, they would immediately take Rosie to the vet. Some veterinarians put after-surgery clothing on the animals, such as belly wraps, T-shirts, and shorts to cover the area that got operated on. Whatever is used, the area must be kept clean, and a topical oint-ment, or medicated cream, may be used to stop swelling and help the healing process. The Bui sisters followed the vet's instructions, making sure Rosie couldn't chew on her stitches.

After two weeks of wearing her lion's mane cone, Rosie was healed and better than ever!

CHAPTER 10
SEED OF AN IDEA

BECAUSE ROSIE AND LILO'S STORY was spreading like wildfire, more and more people were learning not only about Rosie and Lilo, but also about the Bui sisters' unofficial rescue business that they had been running at home for years. And now that business was growing at a very rapid pace!

Although they tried to devote as much time

as they could to helping kittens, Thi, Thoa, and Tram still needed to hold down part-time jobs. They used the money they made to buy supplies: kitten formula, bottles, bottle supplies, heating blankets, kitten food, and more. They were busy but loved nothing more than nursing a kitten back to health and finding them a safe new home.

Thi scrambled around trying to prepare another bottle of kitten formula. Meanwhile, Tram bottle-fed a neonatal kitten and Thoa folded a clean blanket for the next incoming rescue.

"Wouldn't it be great if we had our own office building for the kittens?" Thi asked her sisters, daydreaming about a wonderful space that wasn't located inside their childhood home.

"Yeah," Thoa agreed. "A big facility with lots of volunteers!"

"But we'd need lots of money for that," Tram said, grounding her sisters.

Nevertheless, Thi and her sisters didn't let go of the dream of one day having a kitten rescue headquarters of their own. Securing a physical space would take time and money. The sisters held on to hope. They figured they had to start out somewhere.

"I think if we had a name for the business, it would start to feel real," Thoa suggested.

"Good idea," Tram said. "But what should we call it? A place for our little cats . . ."

The sisters thought and thought. Since they mostly concentrated on rescuing neonatal kittens, the name should probably have something to do with the kittens they were helping. Neonatal kittens were so tiny, and many were sick. How could they put a positive spin on that?

For weeks, Thi, Thoa, and Tram considered lots of names. After many discussions, they came up with the perfect name for their future dream business: Mini Cat Town.

"Now we need a place with a door to hang that name on," Thi said.

"Yeah, and enough money to make our dream become a reality," Tram added.

"Well, we can try saving more of the money that some of Rosie's followers have been donating," Thoa suggested. It was a good idea. Some of Rosie's followers had been donating money to help Rosie and the other foster kittens. The sisters spent all the money they received to cover the costs of caring for the kittens. But they vowed to put some of it aside to save up for their wish of one day opening the wonderful place that they would proudly call Mini Cat Town.

Thi reclined in a chair and laughed as she watched Rosie and Lilo play. She couldn't believe that just a few months ago, Rosie was sick and weak. Now look at her—full of spunk and energy!

Thi leaned down and ruffled Rosie's fur. She was so grateful that she had rescued Rosie and that Rosie had joined their family. Besides all the love Rosie gave them, Rosie had really helped open people's eyes to neonatal kitten rescue. Without publicizing Rosie's story, the sisters wouldn't be getting the generous donations they were saving to open Mini Cat Town.

Lilo came up to Thi and gave her a kiss. "We didn't forget about you, Lilo," Thi said with a lighthearted giggle. "You're so important, too. You are showing the world how to love."

Thi closed her eyes to catch a nap. It had been a long day.

As soon as Thi fell asleep, so did Rosie and Lilo.

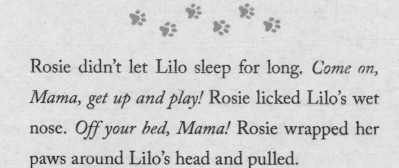

Rosie didn't let Lilo sleep for long. *Come on, Mama, get up and play!* Rosie licked Lilo's wet nose. *Off your bed, Mama!* Rosie wrapped her paws around Lilo's head and pulled.

But Lilo just wanted to stay asleep.

Eyes closed, Lilo opened her mouth and playfully nipped at Rosie.

That's more like it! Rosie nibbled on Lilo's ears and the side of her mouth. *My, what big teeth you have.* Lilo gently batted Rosie—the play fight was on, and Lilo was up and awake.

But Rosie wasn't about to let Lilo get the best of her. She pounced. *Ha! I win!*

"Wake up, sleepyhead," Tram said, walking into Thoa's room early one morning. "It's a beautiful summer day, and I want to go kayaking!"

Thoa pulled her covers up over her head.

"Come on, Thoa, Thi is up and getting Rosie ready for the day," Tram said.

Thoa shot up in bed. "Wait, we're taking Rosie *kayaking*? I mean Lilo and Finny love it, but don't you think she's too . . . *tiny* for that?"

Tram laughed. "It's Rosie we're talking about. You know she's fearless."

In minutes, they were ready to go.

The sisters loaded their bright orange kayak into the lake. A perfect breeze swept over the dock. It was an ideal day to be out on the water. Lilo, wearing her pink life vest, hopped onto the boat. Next, Thi gingerly placed a leashed and life-jacketed Rosie next to her. Would Rosie like the boat? What if she freaked out in the middle of the lake? How would they be able to get her quickly back to shore?

But they knew Rosie wasn't like other cats. She lived for adventures like this one.

Look, Rosie, a big bird! Lilo hung off the edge of the kayak and eyed a goose that was serenely floating by on the clear blue water. Rosie crept next to Lilo to get a closer look. Lilo loved showing Rosie new and exciting things, and this bird was something very new and exciting.

Whoosh! The bird flapped its wings and flew away.

See, Rosie, isn't kayaking the best? We do it all the time! I'm so glad you're here with us today. Rosie meowed in agreement and hung off the side of the boat to take in more of the sights.

"Rosie, you're a natural boater!" Thi said.

"Yeah, she's able to keep her balance and everything," Tram added.

"Where to next, Captain Rosie?" Thoa asked.

This boat is the best! Hey, now let's paddle over there! Rosie pointed with her nose. *And look at all this water! It's like a water* flood *instead of a water fall! Oh, I just love the water so much!*

Rosie leaned closer over the side of the boat as Thi paddled them forward.

Just then, a boat with a motor passed them and . . .

Bump! Jump! Up, down. Up, down.

Wheeee! Riding the waves is so fun!

Yes, Rosie had ridden lots of waves in her short life.

And with Lilo at her side, she was ready to ride a lot more!

CHAPTER 11
TRICKS AND TREATS

GOTCHA! **ROSIE STUCK HER PAW** into the running tap water. *No, I don't gotcha,* she thought as the water ran right through her paws. *What is this stuff, anyway? I remember the lake. Is lake water coming out of the faucet?* Rosie loved chasing moving things. But this water just wouldn't keep still!

Rosie chomped at it. It tasted like water. But Rosie wanted to *catch* it!

She stuck her paws in again and again, but no such luck!

Thi and her sisters found Rosie hilariously playing at the sink, so they posted a video of it online:

We might have a broken kitty, they joked in the caption. *Rosie has recently picked up a weird habit of playing with running water! Thank you for watching!*

Rosie's followers absolutely loved it.

So cute!! She does not fear water at all, she is defo a husky kitty.

"I really do think we have a cat-dog here." Thi scrolled through their latest social media post.

Tram laughed. "Do you think we can teach her tricks, like the ones we've taught Lilo and Finny?"

"Don't laugh," Thoa said, "but I've read that it *is* possible to teach tricks to cats."

Thoa was right: Not only is it good for a cat's well-being to learn tricks, but successfully learning tricks can also heighten a cat's reflexes and keep them active and engaged. Just like teaching a dog new tricks, treats can be used to reward commands. Some people use a clicker to help train their cats. Cats can learn to sit, stand, come, fetch, lie down, high-five, and more!

The sisters needed to figure out the best reward system for Rosie. She didn't like the clicker, and she was very picky about treats. Actually, the *only* treat that Rosie would work for were homemade pumpkin cakes with yogurt frosting or soft-serve ice cream. She loves that they are extra sweet!

Unfortunately for Rosie, those treats were only made for special occasions, so the sisters tried the next best thing.

Using homemade treats, the sisters were able to teach Rosie lots of tricks.

"High-five, Rosie!"

Rosie reached up her front paw and tapped Thi's hand.

"High-ten, Rosie!"

Rosie reached up both front paws and touched Thi's hands.

"Spin!" Tram held a treat in her hand and moved it in a circle.

Rosie spun around and around.

Thoa pointed two fingers at Rosie. "Bang!"

Rosie lay down on her side, still as a statue.

"Kisses?" Thi asked.

Rosie gave Thi a sweet kiss—right on the lips.

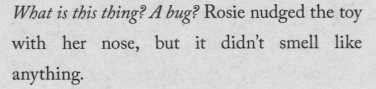

One day, Thi brought home a new toy for Rosie: a pudgy green caterpillar on a set of wheels.

Rosie just stared at the caterpillar.

"Go on, Rosie, play!" Thi urged her.

What is this thing? A bug? Rosie nudged the toy with her nose, but it didn't smell like anything.

But it moved. And it buzzed. Rosie's ears perked up.

Slowly, she walked around the toy. Then she sat down.

I don't think this toy wants to play with me.

Just then, Lilo grabbed the toy with her teeth, and Rosie suddenly wanted to play.

Hey, give it back! she called out to Lilo.

Lilo put the toy back on the ground. While it wasn't traveling along the floor any longer, its wheels were still spinning. Now Rosie was more curious and sniffed the toy again. Its wheels vibrated on her nose, tickling her.

"Here you go, Rosie," Thi said, setting the toy right-side up.

The caterpillar moved, and Rosie batted it with her paws as it moved across the floor.

"See, Rosie? Toys can be fun!" Thi told her with a smile.

"My turn to play!" Tram announced coming into the room, holding Rosie's stuffed kitten (which was actually the same size as Rosie!).

Rosie trotted over and picked up the stuffed cat.

"It's mine!" Tram pulled one end of the stuffed kitty, winking at her sisters.

Rosie pulled back, not wanting to let go. Back and forth, back, and forth, the game of tug-of-war was on. And who won? Rosie, naturally! (Tram couldn't stand to let Rosie lose.)

Next it was time for Rosie to play fetch.

"Go get it!" Tram tossed the stuffed kitty to the other side of the room.

Rosie slid across the wood floor. *Got it!* She carried the toy back.

Tram threw it again, and Rosie quickly retrieved it.

"I think our fans are right," Tram said. "Rosie really is a cat-dog!"

While Rosie learned that playing with toys could be fun, having her teeth brushed was a different matter.

"Open wide!" Thi held out a baby-sized toothbrush with a drop of special cat toothpaste.

Thi knew that it was best to brush a cat's (and a dog's) teeth every day if possible, since mouths have lots of bacteria that can cause tooth decay and gum disease. But Rosie kept her mouth held shut. Tight.

"Come on, girl, this is good for you," Thi said softly.

Rosie gave Thi a look as if saying, *Yeah, right. I've heard that one before! Can't fool me!*

Rosie stared at Thi with her wide green eyes. *No way I'm letting you stick that toothbrush in my mouth.* Rosie's nose twitched, then twitched again. *Wait . . . what's that chicken smell? I LOVE chicken!* She moved her mouth closer to the creamy dollop of stuff that rested on the bristles.

Thi rubbed Rosie's cheeks.

That feels nice . . .

Slowly, Thi put the little toothbrush in Rosie's mouth.

Rosie bit down on the toothbrush and shook her head from side to side.

"You have to let go, Rosie," Thi said. "Otherwise, I won't be able to brush your teeth." Then she glanced over at Lilo. Thoa was brushing her teeth, and Lilo wasn't complaining at all. Which meant Rosie shouldn't be freaking out, either!

Rosie opened her mouth, allowing the toothbrush to move easily over her gums and teeth.

Not bad . . . Not bad at all! And it tastes wonderful!

Tricks, toys, toothbrushes, and now . . . baths! Although cats are good at grooming themselves when they're older, when Rosie was still a kitten, without a mom to groom her, she got her baths in the sink. Tram filled the sink with a few inches of warm water and carefully lowered Rosie in.

"There you go, Rosie, soap and warm water," Tram said. "Who doesn't enjoy a nice bath?"

As if in answer, Rosie meowed and shook her fur.

Bubbles landed all over Tram, but she didn't mind.

Rosie stood up on her hind legs and clung

onto the faucet. But she didn't try to escape! Gently, Tram poured a mug of water over Rosie's fur and added soap. Soon, Rosie was covered in suds! After that, it was time for a rinse, and then towel-drying.

Did Rosie like her bath? It was hard to tell, but she hadn't made a huge fuss!

After posting one of Rosie's baths on YouTube, Rosie's followers were amazed:

I have never seen a cat so calm while getting a bath! She's unbelievably adorable.

I love the look at the end of the video when she has the bubbles on her head. The look is like: Really, Mom, can you put the camera down and hurry up and get me out of here? Haha. The look is priceless.

Priceless indeed!

CHAPTER 12
ROSIE THE MENTOR

ONE DAY, ROSIE WALKED PAST THE gate that separated her, Lilo, and Finny from the kittens the Bui sisters were fostering. Then she turned around. Rosie pressed her nose up to the gate. *They are so tiny.* This was strange behavior, indeed. Rosie had never paid the slightest bit of attention to the rescues before. So why was she interested in them now?

Rosie scratched at the gate, but it didn't open. She wanted in!

Since neonatal kittens are so tiny, Thi, Thoa, and Tram usually kept them separated by a gate from the rest of the animal family. This way, the sisters didn't have to worry about the small kittens getting accidentally hurt by one of the larger animals.

Curious and determined, Rosie looked around, searching for a way to get over the gate. *There are so many kittens! I want to say hi to them all!*

This was a large litter. In fact, this was the largest litter the sisters ever took in: a total of nine kittens! Initially, they were nervous: How could they help each kitten while balancing their schoolwork and jobs? Some of the kittens had to be bottle-fed; others required a dropper on the tongue. And they *all* needed round-the-clock care. If the sisters had their own big place with volunteers, it would be easier. But they were still saving money for that dream. Still, the sisters were determined to do it all, and created a schedule, carving out time to sneak in a few hours of much-needed sleep. Slowly, the kittens began to grow, nourished by milk—and also by love.

Rosie jumped up, but *bam!* She fell right back down.

Then she took a few steps back, ran, and pounced . . . and crashed smack into the gate.

I know I can get over that gate, I just know I can! Rosie thought.

And with that, Rosie took a running start and, with a long leap, cleared the gate!

Hooray! But now what?

A kitten in a green collar crawled up to Rosie and started licking her paw.

Hello, little one. How does my paw taste?

Then another kitten bravely approached.

And you, how does my nose feel? Is it wet?

Rosie lay still as the kittens greeted her. More and more crawled up to her. *Now what do I do?* Then Rosie remembered her earliest days with Lilo, who had been so patient with her. So, that is exactly what Rosie chose to do. Although Rosie didn't have tons and tons of warm fur, she knew that she could still comfort these babies as she cuddled up with them.

"Rosie! How in the world did you get in there?" a shocked Thi asked, opening the gate. It was her turn to feed the kittens, but it looked like Rosie was somehow trying to take her place.

Rosie looked at Thi with her big green eyes.

Thi shook her head. "You know you're not allowed in here." She reached down to try to pick up Rosie, but Rosie wasn't having any of that. She wanted to stay right where she was, curled up with the nine snuggly kittens.

"I've got to get a video of this." Thi pulled out her phone. "Tram and Thoa aren't going to believe it!" After she took a video, Thi quickly fixed the bottles while Rosie lay patiently with the kittens. One by one, Thi picked up the kittens and fed them. When they were done drinking their formula, they went right back to cuddling up with Rosie.

The kittens were falling in love with Rosie, and Thi adored watching Rosie in this new parental role. Rosie, who was usually so full of spunk, lay motionless, letting the kittens snuggle up to her side. Every so often, Rosie let out a *meow* as if to say, *Look at me! I'm a mama, too!*

Lilo walked into the room and looked at Rosie, tilting her head. Was she jealous that Rosie was taking on the parent role? Not at all! She joined in and started licking the kittens' fur!

Thi captured the moment and uploaded the video onto YouTube:

Up until now, Rosie has been indifferent to our 9 new foster kittens. But it looks like Lilo's teachings have rubbed off on her! She started mothering the kittens, and although she has never had a litter of her own, or any milk to give, she is as motherly as they come. ☺ We are so proud of her.

Rosie's fans ate it up:

Thank you for such an adorable and heartwarming moment. I also feel that Lilo's motherly teachings have been imprinted on Rosie!

We could learn so much from these animals!! Love each other and take care of each other, no matter what we look like or how different we may appear.

By leading from example, Rosie and Lilo were spreading very important life lessons!

While Rosie loved all the foster kittens, there was one that she took under her wing more than the rest: Tommy, the green collared kitten who had been the first one to approach Rosie.

"Look at Tommy following Rosie wherever she goes," Thi pointed out.

"Just like Rosie used to follow Lilo . . ." Tram observed.

"Do you think we have another adventure cat on our hands?" Thoa asked.

Thi shrugged. "He could be. Why don't we try taking him out with us? I have to go to the pet store, and Tommy can come along!" Thi held out a black harness for Tommy, and he slid right in—just like Rosie had! Then she leashed up him and Lilo. Tram leashed up Finny, while Thoa put on Rosie's pink harness and leash. And then they were off!

Thi was still nervous taking Lilo to the pet store. She made sure there were no dogs off leash who were near them. She also held firmly on to her leash even though the other animals' leashes were let down—even Tommy's!

At first, Tommy was afraid and crept under a shelf of squeak toys inside the store.

"Tommy!" Tram called, trying to encourage him to come out.

But he stayed put.

"Meow!" Rosie called.

Even that didn't work. Rosie padded over to the shelf and stuck her nose underneath. *Tommy, are you in there?*

When Rosie walked away, Tommy emerged!

"Tommy, you have dust all over you," Thoa said, picking him up and wiping him off.

The sisters laughed. Tommy was so cute, dust ball and all!

Rosie gave him kisses. And Lilo gave her kisses.

Next, it was time to venture outside. Making sure they had a safe place to walk, the sisters took Rosie, Tommy, Lilo, and Finny just outside their house. Using soft, encouraging words, Thi beckoned Tommy to follow along—and that's just what he did.

"Look, Rosie is guarding him!" Thoa observed.

While Lilo walked ahead, Rosie made sure

that Tommy didn't get left behind. When Tommy stopped, Rosie nudged his tail. And when Tommy paused to sniff the grass, so did Rosie. She walked a few paces ahead of him but made sure to turn around to check that he was still there. *Meow!* Rosie was satisfied and walked on, paws padding down the cement sidewalk.

But the next time she turned around, Tommy was nowhere in sight!

"Rosie, where's Tommy?" Tram asked.

Rosie hurried back to try to find him.

Phew! He was just sniffing a bush in front of someone's house.

Rosie waited patiently for him, and then the two padded on.

After a few minutes, Tommy started to feel very brave, and he raced ahead of Rosie. But he soon turned around to make sure Rosie was there, which of course she was! They seemed to have each other's backs . . . just like Lilo had had Rosie's back when she'd been young.

"What do you think about maybe adding Tommy to the pack?" Thi asked as she watched Tommy and Rosie walk down the sidewalk.

"You mean keep him, too? No way," Thoa said. "I mean, I love Tommy and all, but our plates these days aren't just full, they are overflowing!"

"Besides," Tram added, "I already have the perfect home lined up for Tommy. I just have to tell them they'll have an adventure cat on their hands!"

The sun was setting, and day was turning to night. It was time to go home, but Tommy was having too much fun.

"Come on, Tommy, let's go," Thi urged.

When they finally returned home, Tommy curled up and fell asleep nestled in Rosie's fur, her paw gently draped over him.

It was clear Rosie was learning to pay forward the love she had received from Lilo.

CHAPTER 13
ROAD TRIP

"ROAD TRIP!" TRAM CALLED OUT one gorgeous summer afternoon. She excitedly ran through the house, making sure her sisters were awake and getting ready. They were headed to McCloud Falls in Northern California with Rosie, Lilo, and Finny.

"Not so loud, Tram," a sleepy Thoa said. "I know you're excited, but it's still early."

"Yes, but we have to get an early start," Tram reminded her.

The car ride would take about five hours, not including stops, so the sisters had rented a house there to make sure that everyone would be perfectly comfortable once they arrived.

"I think I have everything packed," Thi said, double-checking her list.

When traveling with pets, Thi and her sisters know it's always a good idea to plan ahead. That doesn't mean creating a step-by-step itinerary, but rather figuring out a few things before hitting the road—things that can save time and avoid trouble.

If it's a multi-day trip, the first step is deciding where to stay. For this trip, the sisters rented a house, but they also knew that a cat- and dog-friendly hotel could have been an option. When booking a hotel, they would make sure the hotel allowed pets to be left alone in the room, even if just quickly running out to get food, because some places didn't. The sisters had friends, who when traveling with their pets, stayed in a small pop-up trailer attached to their car. A lot of campgrounds are pet-friendly. With a trailer, pets can be safe and warm and snuggly at night.

"I have the litter boxes, food, bowls, and treats." Thi ticked each one off her list.

"And don't forget baby wipes in case of messes," Tram added.

"And their vaccination records in case we need to make an emergency vet visit," Thoa said.

When everything was checked off the list, Thi, Tram, and Thoa gathered all the pets' supplies (and theirs, too!) and piled into the car.

Rosie and Lilo settled into the back seat of

the car, cozy on a pink, blue, white, and green striped blanket. They were buckled in. The pair were so good together in the car—taking in the scenery out the window and cuddling close together for naps. Of course, just like kids, they did get a bit restless, and this was when the sisters knew it was time for a bathroom and food break!

Once they arrived at their rental house, Rosie and Lilo were eager to get out into the enormous yard. It was a perfect place to run around and stretch their legs after the long ride.

Wait up, Rosie! Lilo raced around the yard as Rosie went wild: up a tree, down a tree, over the grass, through the flowers, up a tree, down a tree, repeatedly. *Slow down, Rosie!* Lilo panted.

Suddenly, Rosie disappeared!

Rosie, where did you go?

Frantically, Lilo looked left and right.

Rosie?

Then she saw something fluffy poking out from a patch of flowers.

There you are, you silly girl!

Rosie was safe, and Lilo was relieved.

McCloud is a hidden jewel, nestled in the slopes of Mount Shasta.

"Wow, look at that," Tram said, gazing up at the fourteen-thousand-foot dark mountain with a volcanic cone on top.

"I hope it doesn't erupt," Thi said, half joking.

"Actually, it's an active volcano," Tram said, reading from her phone. "It says here that it has erupted at least once each eight hundred years over the last ten thousand years."

"What if today is the day?" a nervous Thoa asked.

Tram shrugged. "It could be. The last time it erupted was the year 1250."

Thoa gulped and Thi hugged her. "Don't worry. I think luck is on our side today. Now let's head to the McCloud Waterfalls Trail."

The sisters knew that the trail along the McCloud River would be well paved, making it easy to walk on, especially for Lilo and Rosie. They would pass three beautiful waterfalls and end up in a lush green meadow where the pack could freely frolic.

After hiking for a while, Lilo and Rosie stopped to rest on volcanic rock at the river's edge.

"Photo op!" Thoa said, pulling out her phone and aiming it at Lilo.

Rosie scampered up to sit with Lilo.

"Great shot!" Thoa said.

Once they picked back up and stopped at the lake, they set down their belongings.

"Swimming time!" Tram called out.

"Look at Lilo!" Thi said. "She's not waiting for anyone!"

The sisters laughed as Lilo flew into the lake and doggy-paddled in a circle.

Come on in, Rosie! Lilo said, showing off in the water. *It's fun! I can teach you how to swim.*

Lilo swam back and forth, splashing Rosie when she neared the shore.

Don't be a scaredy-cat, Rosie. I'll be right by your side to protect you!

Rosie was no scaredy-cat. In fact, she tugged on her leash and pulled Thi to the water's edge.

"What do you think?" Thi asked her sisters. "Should we try letting Rosie go in the lake?"

"Well, if you don't, that cute shark life vest you got for her will go to waste," Tram said with a laugh.

Thi nodded and strapped on Rosie's life vest with the shark fin on top. Although she knew Rosie would be safe (and she'd still be holding on to her leash), Thi grew nervous. Rosie had already been to a lake, but she had never been swimming. What if Rosie swallowed too much water as she swam? What if the life vest somehow fell off? Thi shook off her fears and slowly led Rosie into the water. Actually, Rosie led *Thi* into the water!

It became clear that Thi had nothing to worry about. First, Rosie *was* wearing a life vest, which would help keep her afloat. And secondly, swimming is part of a cat's instinctive nature, although a lot of cats avoid swimming at all costs. Similar to their big cat cousins, like lions and tigers, domesticated cats will immediately start paddling their legs if they are in water.

"Look, she's swimming!" Thi called out as Rosie "kitty-paddled" in the lake with Lilo.

"That-a-girl!" Tram said encouragingly.

"This is going to make such a cute video," Thoa said, starting to film.

As Rosie paddled to shore, Lilo was already up and out, dripping on the rocks and waiting. As soon as Rosie got close enough, Lilo grabbed the shark fin to help Rosie ashore.

Thanks, Lilo, but I got this. I don't need your help this time.

See, I can climb up on this rock just fine!

Rosie stopped to shake off water and then continued her way safely onto the shore.

"Good girl!" Tram greeted Rosie on dry land. "I bet you're tired after all that swimming." She bent down to pick her up, but Rosie wiggled away. She already wanted to go back in the lake!

This time, Lilo and Rosie swam side by side, enjoying the cool water under the hot sun.

"Okay, you two," Thi said after a while, "it's time to head back to the house." She waited for Lilo and Rosie to step out of the water, then tried taking off Rosie's life vest.

Rosie wasn't having it. She tried to make a run for it.

Tram giggled. "I guess she wants to keep it on and show it off!"

Rosie pranced proudly down the mountain trail as the pack walked back to the car.

Once they arrived back at their rental house, Rosie wanted to have even more fun. She raced around the yard and up and down the trees. Lilo, on the other hand, was tired, as were Thi, Thoa, and Tram.

"Come on, Rosie, time to go inside for dinner," called Thi.

Rosie scampered inside the house, where they all had a good, hearty meal.

After eating, Rosie and Lilo curled up on a cozy red blanket and fell fast asleep.

CHAPTER 14
IT'S STILL CHRISTMAS WITHOUT SNOW

CHRISTMAS WAS RIGHT AROUND the corner, but Thi, Tram, and Thoa knew not to expect snow.

The temperatures in San Jose, California, average between forty-two and eighty-two degrees, so it's not cold enough for snow there, although it does get an average of seventeen inches of rain per year! December,

January, and February are its rainiest months.

Thoa loved to snowboard, and while it didn't snow in San Jose, the sisters did travel up to the mountains where there was lots of snow. "I really want to hit the slopes," she said.

"Me too," said Tram. "I mean it *is* December."

The sisters promptly took a trip to Lake Tahoe. While Lilo and Finny loved the snow, Rosie tiptoed around, not sure what to make of the cold stuff beneath her paws. As she tried to keep up with the pack, she shook her paws to try to get the snow off.

This stuff is cold. And sticks to my fur. Help! Get it off me! It's too cold!

Lilo turned around to see why it was taking Rosie so long to catch up.

Rosie sat in the snow shivering.

Can we go home now? Please?

Poor Rosie was not cut out for snow trekking after all. But the pack knew they could still have a merry Christmas without snow.

On Christmas morning, Thi, Thoa, and Tram posted a video with a heartfelt message:

Our pack wishes everyone a Merry Christmas! We are extremely grateful for such an incredible year. And we owe it to all our wonderful followers (supporting us with our independent foster program, fixing of feral cats, and even adopting every single kitten!). Thank you so much from the bottom of our hearts; we could not have done it without you!

The video showed Lilo, Finny, and Rosie under the Christmas tree, surrounded by colorfully wrapped gifts. Finny chewed on a new toy. Lilo pawed at the wrapping paper of her gift, determined to unwrap it. Rosie, wearing a red velvet bow around her neck, sniffed a small box with snowmen-patterned wrapping and a shiny gold ribbon. She didn't know where to start. When she grabbed a corner of the box in her mouth, she dropped it as quickly as she lifted it!

A shiny, pretty thing! Rosie pawed at the bow that sat atop the box. *I want to play!* Rosie pawed and pawed. The bow popped off and stuck to her nose! *This is fun, fun, fun! I love this holiday!*

As Rosie toyed with her bow, Lilo got to work opening Rosie's *actual* gift.

Thi, Thoa, and Tram knew that their own best gifts were right in front of them: Lilo, Rosie, and Finny. They felt grateful to be a part of this sweet and loving pack. If they had one Christmas wish, it was that they could get their own space for Mini Cat Town one day soon.

The seed of an idea they had last year was sprouting, with donations coming in, but it had yet to flourish and become a reality. The sisters weren't giving up, though, and they weren't wishing for it to magically happen. They would keep working hard until their dream came true.

CHAPTER 15
ROSIE GOES VIRAL

ROSIE AND LILO CONTINUED TO gain followers, supporters, and donors on social media. Soon, Rosie and Lilo's tale began appearing in other places, which thrilled Thi, Thoa, and Tram!

That summer, *Love Meow*, a website that covers impactful and meaningful cat and kitten stories, featured Rosie. Even *The Daily*

Mail in the United Kingdom and one of Australia's leading news websites published stories about the unique relationship between Rosie and Lilo.

The unlikely friendship tale between cat and dog was spreading across the world.

That winter, ABC News did a story, too. Thoa, who was interviewed, explained how they had found Rosie as a sick kitten. She added: "We took a chance and put her with Lilo, and Lilo really saved her life. Lilo never left Rosie's side for hours. She cuddled her and comforted her until she was better and finally ready to drink from a bottle."

Just like the sisters' posts, this story received lots of comments:

These are the stories that make life normal. We need more like this.

Kudos to the Buis. They are obviously some pretty special people and amazing pet parents. Very uplifting story.

People around the world were craving uplifting stories like the one about Rosie and Lilo. The love growing between the two animals was just too amazing and heartwarming not to share!

On May 28, 2016, even more people were about to find out about Rosie and Lilo.

"Mom, can you please grab the popcorn?" Tram called from the living room. "And some drinks, too?" she added.

"Um, just because you're about to become a TV star doesn't mean that Mom is your personal assistant now," Thoa said with a wink.

"Sorry," Tram said. "I just want to get the TV to the right channel, because . . ."

"In a few minutes, we will be on TV!" Thi finished her sister's sentence. Today was the day that their segment on National Geographic's *Unlikely Animal Friends* was finally airing.

"It's on! It's on!" Tram jumped up and down.

Thi pulled her sister down to the couch. "Settle," she joked, using the same word she used for their pets.

Thi picked up Rosie and placed her in her lap. "You're about to become famous!"

In moments, their faces filled the TV screen, with the narrator talking all about Rosie and Lilo. The sisters squealed and tried to contain their excitement as Thoa appeared for her big interview moment. No one took their eyes off the TV until the segment was over.

"I'm so proud of us," Thoa said, turning to her sisters.

"Me too," said Tram.

"And I'm so proud of *you*, Thoa," Thi said. "You came across so well."

Thoa beamed. "Why, thank you!"

Thanks to the National Geographic show, the sisters (and Rosie and Lilo) had gained even *more* followers! Then, in August, *The Dodo* published an article on Rosie and Lilo. *The Dodo* is known for sharing heartwarming, uplifting animal stories and videos that go viral and reach people around the world. Today, *The Dodo* receives over *two billion* views per month!

The Dodo interviewed Thoa for their article, and she relayed the story of how Thi found Rosie and how Lilo helped nurse Rosie back to health. The article read: "And little by little, the dewy-eyed kitten awakened to her new world—a world where motherhood isn't bound by species."

Thoa explained: "She definitely has her cat-like features, because she has other cats living in the house who are her friends as well, but I think she knows deep down inside that she was raised by a husky. And she takes on so many of those features. She thinks she's more a dog than anything."

The article ended with: "You might forgive Rosie for fancying herself a dog. After all, when all the human kindness in the world couldn't substitute for a mother's love, a dog stepped up. And that dog has been by her side ever since."

"Oh my gosh, I can't believe this!" Thoa shouted one morning.

"Don't tell me," Thi said, running into her room. "You just got a call for Rosie and Lilo to be featured on another television show?"

Thoa shot up in bed. "How did you know?!"

"Wait, really?" Thi said. "I was just joking because that's what *I* said when I got that message about filming for National Geographic."

Tram shook her head. "I can't believe you remember your exact words."

Thi rolled her eyes. "Well, it was an exciting moment. My reaction is etched in my memory!"

"Enough, you two," Thoa gently scolded. "Don't you want to hear the news?"

"Sorry," Thi and Tram said at the same time.

"*The Dodo* wants to film us for an episode of their *Comeback Kids* series!" Thoa announced.

Thi pulled out her phone and scrolled through it until she found some information on the videos. "It says here that 'These animals had a rough start in life—until they found someone who refused to give up on them.'"

"That would be us!" Tram said.

"Especially Lilo," Thi added.

"So, do you think we are up for another video shoot?" Thoa asked her sisters.

Thi and Tram nodded. They were all in agreement.

Thoa grinned. "*Comeback Kids*, here we come!"

The Bui sisters weren't exactly experts at filming, but at least this time they knew what to expect.

On the day of this filming, the sisters woke up early and took the dogs for a run to get out any nervous jitters or anxiety. Then they gathered up the pack and drove about an hour to a kayaking center, on a lake in Sausalito, California, where the filming would take place.

When they reached the kayak center, the owner remarked that he had never had a cat in one of his kayaks.

But there's a first time for everything, right?

"Lilo and Rosie need to be on the same boat together," Thoa explained. "Otherwise, Lilo starts to freak out."

Thi and Tram helped put Rosie, who was wearing a matching shark life vest with Lilo, into Thoa's orange kayak and pushed them out into the water. Soon, Thi and Tram were paddling alongside them in a yellow kayak with Finny. The film crew took boats of their own.

Lilo rested her paws on the front of the boat, checking out their surroundings.

Suddenly, Lilo slipped!

"Lilo, you okay?" a concerned Thoa asked.

But it was just her front paws that had slipped. Lilo was fine. Meanwhile, Rosie didn't seem too concerned about Lilo. She was much more interested in the sights.

Rosie hung over the edge of the kayak, feeling the wind rustling in her fur.

Ah, the water and the breeze are wonderful! This is the life! Rosie sat at the front of the kayak with Lilo, taking in the view. The boats at port. The rolling hills dotted with homes. *What's that over there? I want to get a closer look!* Rosie crept closer to the boat's edge, and then—

SPLASH!

She fell straight into the water.

Rosie! Lilo panicked. *I'll rescue you!* But she didn't have to leap to the rescue. Rosie looked calm floating in the water, safe in her life jacket—no need to worry here!

And an instant later, Thoa pulled Rosie safely back into the boat.

Phew! Thank goodness for Thoa and leashes—and shark vests!

"You okay, Rosie?" Thoa asked as Rosie shook off drops of water.

Rosie looked at her as if saying: *Of course. I can take care of myself. I'm all grown up now!*

"Rosie, you were a real shark there for a while!" one of the producers joked.

Once everyone was back on the dock,

Thoa told Lilo and Rosie's story from the beginning. "Rosie's all grown up," Thoa explained. "She's much more independent from Lilo. And Lilo's still kind of holding on to that motherhood. So Lilo will clean her, and Rosie will just have to tolerate it. But she still needs Lilo there sometimes to support her."

"I can't believe this," Thoa said, scrolling through her phone.

"What can't you believe?" Tram asked.

"There are *thousands* of likes of *The Dodo* video of Rosie and Lilo!"

"Like, thousands more than the likes we get on our videos?" Tram asked.

Thoa nodded.

"You're not going to believe this," Thi said, coming into the room just then.

"We know," Thoa said, holding up her phone.

"Wow, Rosie's story has really gone viral this time!"

"I mean, *The Dodo* does have a lot of followers—a lot more than we do," Tram said.

"In fact," Thoa said, "our follower count just went way up. And it keeps on increasing!"

Thi held up her hand. "Wait. Our social media followers aren't that important. I mean they are, because we're bringing attention to Rosie and Lilo. But people are starting to understand that differences can only make you stronger, that differences can bring people together."

"You're right," Thoa said. "Thank you, Rosie and Lilo!"

CHAPTER 16
GRAND OPENING

"THERE IS A LINE OF AT LEAST ONE hundred people out there!" a breathless Thi reported as she ran through the door of Mini Cat Town.

Tram jumped for joy. "I can't believe we did it. The day of our grand opening is here!"

"And people are actually lined up to get inside!" Thoa added.

The sisters walked through their four-thousand-square-foot facility, one part kitten lounge and one part adoption center, making sure that they were ready to welcome their crowd of eager visitors.

"I'm so proud of the job you did putting this place together," the sisters' mom said as her daughters led her through the facility.

And their mom was right: Mini Cat Town looked amazing! The kitten lounge was filled with comfy chairs and couches for the humans, and lots of climbing structures, scratching posts, and toys for the cats.

The adoption center part of the floor, had portable gates where potential adopters could sit and safely play with the kittens.

Thi fluffed up a pillow on a couch in the lounge, while Thoa rearranged the cat toys.

"So, are we ready?" Tram asked as she folded a colorful blanket.

The sisters nodded, and Tram opened the door.

Everyone outside cheered and started coming in.

"Here we, go!" Thi said, greeting their guests with a huge smile.

"Everyone has to fill out a waiver before entering," Thoa instructed. "And adults, please fill one out for the kids you are with."

After the waivers were filled out, each person was handed a pair of plastic slippers to place over their shoes to prevent tracking in dirt and mud. Adults paid fifteen dollars for thirty minutes, and ten dollars for children eleven years and under.

Once inside, it was playtime! Each group got their own area where they played with the kittens, who wore colorful collars with their names written on them. If people didn't feel like playing with a kitten, they held or cuddled one!

Thi looked at her sisters and their mom, and grinned. They had worked hard and made their dream come true. Their mom was so proud of them.

A banner hung inside the lounge, which would note how many kittens had been adopted from Mini Cat Town. Thi and her sisters hoped that number would get bigger every day! Another banner in the room reads: BE PAWSITIVE. And there was space on another wall to show photos of all the kittens who are available for adoption in case one captures someone's heart.

In the cat lounge, there were a few key rules visitors needed to follow:

- Let the kitten come to you. Don't chase the kittens, or you may scare them. Although it is not permitted to pick up the cats, a volunteer can do so and put him or her in your lap.
- Be gentle with the kittens. Pet them softly, and definitely don't pull on their tails!
- If a cat is sleeping or eating, please don't bother them.
- Don't feed the kittens, and don't bring in any food for yourself, either. Only water is allowed.
- Use indoor voices. Loud noises can frighten the kittens.
- It's okay to take pictures as long as you remember to turn off your flash.

On opening day, Thi noticed a little girl sitting on the floor with her grandmother. The girl looked sad: No kittens were coming to her.

Thi picked up a kitten with a pink collar and gently placed him in the little girl's lap. "Here you go," Thi said. "Sometimes the kittens are just shy."

"Just like you," the girl's grandmother said sweetly.

Thi escorted the little girl and her grandmother to the adoption floor to meet even more kittens. There, the kittens were cared for by volunteers until they could find their forever homes. Mini Cat Town couldn't be run without its volunteers, who do everything from bottle-feeding and washing the blankets to sanitizing the space and keeping the kittens company!

In the weeks that followed the grand

opening, Mini Cat Town had many events with prospective adopters who sat in a pen with the adorable kittens. If they fell in love with a kitten, they could fill out an application to take the cat home. The sisters only accepted an application if they were sure that the kitten would be treated with kindness and respect in their new home.

When one was adopted, the sisters felt good that the kitten would be cared for and loved.

By the end of Mini Cat Town's grand opening, the sisters were exhausted.

"This is unbelievable," Thi said, checking the registration book. "We had 650 guests!"

"Wow!" Tram exclaimed.

"And 21 adoptions," Thoa added.

Thoa, Thi, and Tram gathered up the kittens and placed them in their assigned playpens along with their litter mates. Each playpen had everything the kittens needed: wet food, dry food, a litter box, and a comfy blanket.

"Why do you have to put the kittens in their playpens at night?" a volunteer asked.

"Having kittens in a playpen in the evening gives the kittens a chance to rest," Thoa explained. "And when they are on the floor, they know they will come back to a safe and comfortable place at the end of the day."

The volunteer nodded. "That makes total sense."

The sisters thanked their wonderful volunteers and bid them good night.

"I'm sure tomorrow will be another busy day," Thi said.

"Yup," Tram agreed. "Especially since we

decided to open smack in the middle of kitten season."

Kitten season is the time of year, usually between March and October, when cats often have babies. A female cat is pregnant for eight-and-a-half weeks before giving birth. That's not very long compared to a human pregnancy, which lasts about forty weeks! A cat usually gives birth to a litter of around four kittens. If these kittens are born on the street, they add to the growing feral cat population.

Rosie was born on the street and left as an orphan, but she was also neonatal and required special care. Every year during kitten season, thousands of orphaned neonatal kittens are moved into shelters. Sadly, most shelters are short-staffed and do not have enough people to provide the same round-the-clock care as the Bui sisters did for Rosie. That's why

Thi, Thoa, and Tram have worked so hard to rescue kittens on their own. They also work alongside the San Jose Animal Care Center, which gets five thousand orphaned kittens a year! Those that weigh less than one pound can't survive without proper care. This is where Thi, Thoa, and Tram—and Mini Cat Town— come in.

As soon as the sisters returned home from Opening Day, Lilo and Rosie bolted over to them.

Where have you been all day? Lilo wondered.

Why do you smell like other cats? Rosie wanted to know.

"Aw, did you miss us?" Thi gave Rosie and Lilo a hug. "We were off doing very important work today!"

Important work indeed! What began as the seed of an idea only a few years ago had finally been realized. The sisters now had a dedicated space outside their home to run their business. This was only able to happen through generous donations made by fans and followers of the sisters' social media accounts showcasing Rosie and Lilo.

Now Thi, Thoa, and Tram's work to rescue and nurse neonatal kittens could continue on a larger scale. They could take in more than one litter at a time, nurse kittens back to health, and find them loving homes, all with Rosie and Lilo by their sides. They were a family, a pack—and they knew they always would be.

CHAPTER 17
EPILOGUE

TO THIS DAY, ROSIE AND LILO remain the best of friends. They enjoy their sunny walks, kayak trips, and hilly hikes. (Except Rosie still isn't so thrilled about the snow!) Rosie loves sticking her head out the window on long car rides and feeling the wind rushing through her fur. But even best friends have to discover what it is like to be an individual.

Recently, Rosie went hiking with Lilo, Finny, Miko, and their cousin DJ. The day was cool and crisp, and the sun was bright in the sky.

As Rosie followed along, she got bored watching the dogs running. She crept into the shadows to find some fun of her own.

Rosie sniffed and sniffed, her ears perked up and her bushy tail wagged.

Yum! This stick is crunchy! And this blade of grass is so smooth.

Lilo wandered over to her. *What's so interesting, Rosie?*

Rosie looked up at Lilo, and then turned back to sniffing and exploring.

Lilo was beginning to understand that Rosie had grown up. Even though Rosie didn't need her as much anymore, Lilo knew her love for this adventure cat would never fade.

After returning home and eating dinner, Lilo settled down in her bed. She looked for Rosie, but she was busy playing with Thi.

Why isn't Rosie as tired as me? Why doesn't Rosie want to go to bed?

Lilo sighed and closed her eyes.

But just as she was falling asleep, Rosie walked over and snuggled right next to her. Lilo peeked open one eye.

I love when Rosie snuggles with me.

The two animals cozied up together in their soft, warm bed. Rosie may have gotten older, but that didn't mean she didn't want to be with Lilo anymore. Lilo had kept Rosie safe as a kitten and taught her how to take risks, try new things, and have adventures. Even though Rosie was all grown up, Rosie and Lilo knew their strong bond would never be broken. That's because they would always be more than best friends. They were family.

MORE ABOUT MINI CAT TOWN

What began as three sisters feeding stray cats outside their home led to the creation of an independent rescue and nonprofit rescue organization with over two hundred volunteers, forty foster homes, and seven board members! Since its grand opening, Mini Cat Town has rescued over one thousand cats and kittens.

Mini Cat Town gives the kittens' foster parents all the supplies they need to care for the kittens. Every two weeks, the fosters bring the kittens back to Mini Cat Town for a routine checkup. At the checkups, the kittens are dewormed and given flea treatments. They also get their shots. If there's an emergency, Mini Cat Town helps out with that, too. And once the kittens are old enough, Mini Cat Town pays for them to be spayed or neutered, and for a microchip to track the kittens in case they get lost.

When the kittens have recovered from surgery, the fosters can bring them back to Mini Cat Town for follow-up care. Besides regular checkups and shots, the kittens are also weighed daily. This is important to make sure they're growing up just as they should be— happy and healthy!

Thi, Thoa, and Tram have made it their business to not only rescue as many kittens as they can, but to give them the best care possible! Now, a bit more about the sisters:

Thi, one of Mini Cat Town's cofounders, graduated from San Jose State University with a degree in biomedical engineering. But instead of finding a job in her field, she decided to focus on rescuing kittens. She is the president of the board of directors and manages Mini Cat Town's volunteer program. Thi has been passionate about kitten rescue for as long as she can remember, and she still has that first rescue she brought into her house over fifteen years ago—a short-haired brown tabby named Sparky. In her free time, Thi likes hiking with Lilo and Rosie, snowboarding, and overseas travel.

Thoa, the middle Bui sister, is a graduate of the University of California, Davis, and another cofounder of Mini Cat Town. She is the adoption coordinator for Mini Cat Town and runs all their social media. She is also the treasurer for the board of directors. Thoa has always been passionate about rescuing kittens and has a soft spot for rehabilitating special needs kittens in particular. In her spare time, Thoa likes to travel, snowboard, and work on short films.

Tram, the third cofounder and youngest Bui sister, has a love for all animals and a passion for animal rescue—not just for cats and kittens. She works at the San Jose Animal Care Center as a kitten coordinator. There, she finds foster families to care for the neonatal kittens. She is also Mini Cat Town's foster coordinator. Tram graduated from San Jose State University with a degree in biological sciences and a minor in chemistry. When she's not working with kittens, Tram loves to travel, read, or Rollerblade with her dog, Finny.

In a message on their website, the sisters

wrote: "Looking to adopt? Rescue a kitten! We believe big changes start with small efforts and our combined efforts today can change the world tomorrow. Ask yourself how you can advocate for a kitten today."

For more information, visit the Mini Cat Town website: minicattown.org.

HOW TO TRAIN
AN ADVENTURE CAT

Thoa has some tips on how to train your cat if they want to be an adventure cat like Rosie:

1. LEASH AND HARNESS TRAINING:

You need three things to get started: a standard "H" harness, a leash that attaches to the harness, and your cat's favorite treats. You can find any of these items at your local pet store. Next, you need to help your cat get used to the harness by rewarding them each time the harness is on and helping them associate good things with the harness every time it is on. So, put the harness on during mealtime, treat time, and playtime.

2. OUTDOOR ADVENTURES: To get your cat used to going outdoors, say lots of encouraging words. Pay attention to your cat's body language: An upright tail means your cat has lots of confidence! If your cat stops to shake for a second or two, don't worry, it just means they are shaking off nerves—after all, being outside is a new experience for your cat. But if your cat is really shivering, it is time to bring them back inside. Always reward your cat for being outdoors so they will associate being outdoors with good things. Your cat's willingness to eat shows they are comfortable. Don't be afraid to explore new places: Take your cat to the beach, out on the snow, or up a mountainside if they seem to enjoy visiting these places. Leave lots of time for your cat to sniff around and explore! And when your cat gets tired, simply carry them!

3. HAVE PATIENCE: Show your cat that it's okay to be outdoors and that there can be more to life than sitting inside all day looking through the window. However, some cats are homebodies (just like humans), and you should never push your cat to do something they don't love. If your cat's favorite place in the whole world is your sofa, embrace it—and curl up there together!

LEND A HELPING HAND

There are lots of ways that you can help feral cats, stray cats, and shelter cats. Some you can do on your own, while others may require help from an adult:

VOLUNTEER AT AN ANIMAL SHELTER. Many shelters require volunteers to be a certain age, so you might need to wait a few years or ask for an adult's help. At a shelter, you can do many jobs: walk dogs, clean out litter boxes, refill water bowls, give out treats, and simply play with the animals to help them get used to people before being adopted. Sharing your love with animal shelter residents goes a long way!

RAISE MONEY. There are lots of animal organizations that need money to buy supplies, rescue more animals, build enclosures, and more. It can be overwhelming to find the perfect place to help, so why not start by looking at ones in your town? Is there a local rescue organization or shelter that could use your help? Once you find the right place, it's time to figure out how to raise money to donate. Here are some suggestions:

- Organize a bake sale and sell the baked goods in a public place, like outside your house, in front of your school, or even at the library. Be sure to get permission from the place you're selling before setting up, and always make sure to talk to an adult before organizing anything!

- Set up a loose change jar in your house. Sometimes, people have loose change lying around that they aren't using, so why not ask your family members and visitors to drop it in a jar designated for donations?

- When it's your birthday or the holidays, ask friends and family to donate money to the shelter you are supporting.

COLLECT OLD BLANKETS AND SHEETS.

Shelters are often in need of blankets, sheets, and towels to keep their animals warm and clean. Ask friends and families if they have any extras, then bring the clean donations to the animal shelter. (Always call first to make sure they are currently accepting donations.)

ADOPTION IS AMAZING! Since there are so many cats and kittens in shelters, it is a fantastic idea to adopt a cat. Even if you aren't planning to adopt a cat yourself, you can still encourage your friends and family to do so.

FOSTER. If you and your family are not ready to welcome a forever cat or kitten into your home, you might want to try fostering. Some animals only need fostering for a few days, others a few months. Talk to your family and someone at an animal shelter to see what you can do to help.

BE KIND. Above all else, always be kind to animals. Show them love, and they will return that love a million times over!

CARING FOR YOUR KITTEN

Just like how parents babyproof the house before a new baby is brought home, you will have to kittenproof before bringing a new forever friend home. Your new kitten will be curious, so be sure to put away small objects such as pens and pencils, small toys or toy pieces, jewelry, paper towels, toilet paper, rubber bands, and hair accessories. Also, make sure that any cords in your house are bundled or stowed in a drawer. And make sure all toilet bowl lids and cabinets doors are shut.

You will also have to shop for supplies, such as these items:

- Food bowl
- Water bowl
- Kitten food
- Kitten treats
- Litter box
- Litter
- Scratching post
- Cat bed
- Thick blanket
- Toys
- Grooming brush
- Nail clipper
- Cat carrier
- Collar with ID tag

Once you bring your kitten home, it will take them time to adjust to their new surroundings, so remember to have patience. If your kitten seems shy at first, just open the door to their carrier. Even the shyest of kittens eventually comes out to say hi! But give them the space to do so on their own terms.

Your kitten may want to hide away when they first arrive, and you should give them all the time they need to get used to your place. It just takes a while for you to earn their trust! (But make sure you keep an eye on them so you know where they are, even if they're hiding in the closet.) You probably will want to show them off to all your family and friends right away, but instead, slowly introduce your kitten to new people to give them time to learn everyone's touch and smell. Too much too soon will be overwhelming.

If someone wants to pick up your kitten, make sure they do it properly, with one hand behind their front legs and the other hand under their backside. And if there are any small children in your house, make sure they don't tug on your kitten's ears, tails, or whiskers!

Once your kitten has explored their new home, it is best to create a space for them in the house for when you're not there. This place should have a cat bed, litter box, and food and water bowls. This might be a gated-off kitchen or an enclosed section of a room. Make sure the room has a floor that can be cleaned up easily.

Your kitten needs energy to grow, so make sure you feed them food specially made for kittens. And remember that kittens can be finicky: They might not eat all their food at once, so just keep it in their bowl so they can nibble a little at a time.

Kittens will instinctively bury their poop, but your kitten might not know exactly *where* to do this, so you will have to show them where their litter box is located. The best time to do this is after they've had a meal or a treat. You might have to take their paw and help them dig in the litter or rustle the litter a bit with your hands. If you see your kitten pee or poop in the box, praise them immediately so they connect this behavior with good things. You can even offer them a treat!

Brushing your kitten's fur and trimming their nails is a good habit to get into, and it's a good idea to start this right away so that they will get used to this activity. Clipping their nails will help prevent their claws from getting caught on something. (Make sure you buy a special set of nail clippers for kittens.) And brushing their fur will not only help keep it shiny, but will also help prevent excess fur from falling out as fur balls (which your kitten can gag on!).

As soon as you can, bring your kitten to the vet. Discuss with your vet what you have been feeding your kitten and their general behavior and well-being at home. Your vet will give you a vaccine schedule and will discuss the proper time for spaying or neutering.

Above all, give your kitten lots of cuddles and love! They're so lucky they have you to make their life better—and guess what? They're going to make yours better, too!